TSUNAMI PRESS 1

Bookstore Clerks
& Significant Others

TSUNAMI PRESS 1

Editor: SCOTT LANDFIELD

Associate Editor: S.G. ELLERHOFF

Cover Artist: EMILY POOLE

Cover Design by Claire Flint Last

TSUNAMI PRESS
EUGENE, OREGON

TSUNAMI PRESS 1 is the first in a series of anthologies published by Tsunami Press, the publishing branch of Tsunami Books. Since 1995, Tsunami Books has been a Bookstore and Community Events Center in Eugene, Oregon.

Tsunami Press
2585 Willamette Street
Eugene, Oregon 97405

www.tsunamibooks.org

Some material in this anthology was previously published elsewhere:
Elly Bookman's "Code Red" first appeared in *Bennington Review* (Issue 9, Sep. 2021).
S.G. Ellerhoff's illustration for "The Fox & the Hedgehog" makes use of Elizabeth Murray's watercolor landscape "Wicklow Hills" from 1843.
Nina Kiriki Hoffman's "Escapes" first appeared in 2002 in *Shelf Life*, an anthology published by Dreamhaven Books, a Minneapolis bookstore run by Greg Ketter.
Carter McKenzie's "A brutal theory of the fetal heartbeat" was originally published in *Tikkun Magazine*, 22 Dec. 2022.
Erik Muller's *A Boy's Eyes* was originally published by Placeholder Press, 2011.
Jenny Root's "That Which Lies Beside the Slough" was previously published in *About Place Journal: Dignity as an Endangered Species in the 21st Century* (Vol. V, Issue 3, May 2019); "Eclipse and Fire" previously published in *Fireweed* (Summer 2021).
John Witte's "Prose" (as "Oh Well") and "Poetry" were previously published in *All That Matters Now* (Lynx House Press, 2023).
Kelsey Yoder's "Ocean Bound" was previously published in *Five Points* (Vol. 18, Issue 1, Spring 2017).

ISBN 979-8-9881512-0-3 (paperback)

Printed in the United States of America.

FIRST PRINTING

CONTENTS

INTRODUCTION IX

D.S. Rhodes
THE SECRET BOOKSHOP 1

Jenny Root
RENASCENT... 13
THAT WHICH LIES BESIDE THE SLOUGH 14
ECLIPSE AND FIRE... 16

Dorianne Laux
DRIVING THROUGH THE AVENUE OF THE GIANTS
    VIA THE TRINITY RIVER BYWAY 17
REDWOODS 18
UNDERSTORIES.. 20

Joseph Millar
ART MUSEUM 21
ANTOINETTE 23
CHAPTER 13.. 24

Matthew Dickman
LEVELING UP 25
PARENTAL DREAM 35
A PASSING 38

Kelsey Yoder
OCEAN BOUND 41

Michael McGriff
EXCERPTS FROM A BOOK-LENGTH POEM, INQUEST...................... 55

Maxine Scates
    FALLING 61
    WAYS OF SEEING 63
    APRIL 65
    ONGOING 67

Meli Hull
    NON-WORDS 71

Ken Babbs
    FARM LIFE 74

Eve Müller
    NOTES FROM MY FATHER'S BEDSIDE 80

Erik Muller
    A BOY'S EYES, { A POEM } 85

Carter McKenzie
    A BRUTAL THEORY OF THE FETAL HEARTBEAT 118
    CALLING FOR HIS MOTHER 122

Tom Titus
    ON THE LAM 125

Jorah LaFleur
    I WRITE 130

Nina Kiriki Hoffman
    ESCAPES 133

Bob Craven
    ODE TO A DOG, HIT BY A BEER TRUCK 150
    "ETERNAL MYSTERY" 152

Cecelia Hagen
    SHELL GAME 153
    LOVE SONG FOR A LONG MARRIAGE 154

Valerie Ihsan
  EYE CONTACT.. 155

Brian Cutean
  THAT ZEBRA LOOK 163
  CRAZY PEOPLE.. 165

Bronwynn Dean
  HYDRO SOLILOQUY 167

Mose Tuzik Mosley
  FLOCK OF BIRDS.. 169

Deb Casey
  AUTO-CORRECT 180
  FOUR DRESSES
    YOUR FASHION-FORWARD SISTERS ARE RAVING OVER....... 181

John Witte
  PROSE 182
  POETRY 183

S.G. Ellerhoff
  THE FOX & THE HEDGEHOG 184

Elly Bookman
  WHITE COLLAR 203
  POEM 205
  CODE RED 207

Scott Landfield
  AN OLD-TIME LOCAL-INTEREST STORY................................. 209

CONTRIBUTORS.. 221

INTRODUCTION

I'm seated at a cafe table salvaged from the old Tango Center, next to a 1920 Mason & Hamlin grand piano originally built in Boston, owned in Eugene by Victor Steinhardt, then rebuilt over the past few months by Rick Carter. It was played tonight for the first time in its new life by a thirty-six-year-old refugee from Saint Petersburg named Andrei Andreev, one of the great pianists in the world. There was a small crowd, a perfect audience, who shared an experience we will remember. When I'm done with this note I will mop and vacuum the floor, clean the bathrooms, do everything needed to turn this concert hall back into a Bookstore, then go home and prepare for another day of work.

The table is up on the stage at Tsunami Books, a 4,000-square-foot cement block building with a barrel roof on Willamette Street in beautiful South Eugene, Oregon, built in 1949 to provide wallpaper and curtains for the booming populace beginning to people the hills surrounding this end of Eugene Skinner's town. I built this stage, along with friend Chris Cassidy—my handball teammate in high school in Illinois—who was a hell of a builder, and still is, when he gets his old body going. At the time, twenty-five years ago, I was a highly experienced "grunt" laborer, mostly in the mountains, who was good at doing the workload of two or more in a day. At forty-four, the damage I'd done to my body promised to be permanent. I stumbled into the idea of owning a Bookstore, like each of my long-dead parents had at desperate moments of their own. The whim to build a stage by the two windows at the back of the building included the intention to finish writing the books obsessively begun.

Suddenly, here I am, a sixty-nine-year-old clerk, working seventy hours a week to cover the high rent and low wages required for the opportunity to experience the wondrous organic process of the growing of a Bookstore and Community Events Center, and now a Press, in a neighborhood full of remarkable people; all these years doing the daily tasks of two or more good workers at a completely different job. Builder, buyer and seller of books, impresario, clerk, scholar, janitor, goat, catch-all, principled pauper, a dozen gigs under the same roof, the writing relegated to endless beginnings, note-books piled on the desk in the rented cabin up the hill. The focus it would take to write a real book while working endless hours fifty-two weeks a year, every month the same scrap for rent. . . Well, I think it would have killed me to try. And I really want to live.

Which is to say, thanks to Tsunami Books for giving me good reason to live a long good life. Thanks to the million or more curi-ous, educated people who have come through the door, always with the best of manner and intent. Thanks to the 5,000 wondrous official events that have occurred here. Thanks to the countless daily un-official events. Thanks to walking the aisles late at night, gazing at the books in the half light. Thanks to the patina that deepens the colors of the soul that shepherds these moments, Tsunami Books a big umbrella for the arts and the human heart. Everywhere out there the storms rage, but from here it's just another rainbow over a Bookstore with a new roof in a land of good rain.

Thanks to the many, many people who daily say "hang in there," who then back their words with books bought and sold, show tickets purchased, and occasionally just wads of bills flung with smiling nonchalance across the wide plank counter. The stories I could tell of the people who have kept this Bookstore, and along the way, me, alive, would fill a book I promise to rewrite from the stories written on the stage on nights like this.

And yes, a twisted thanks to the COVID, which brought in a few government dollars, and an extra purpose to continue, getting books to the people, so they could hunker down and pass long, quiet hours just staying alive, reading. Thanks, too, to the COVID, which brought Dr. Steve stumbling through, someone with the desire and knowledge, and cavalier energy to help start a Press, which has been a dream forever here at Tsunami. It actually began, Tsunami Press, in the heart of the COVID, a great fun collaborative affair with Sky-pilot Ken Babbs, who had seventy-one remembrances waiting to fit into a well-built book.

And now here we are, a new press in a new era, both good reasons to keep an old Bookstore alive, to keep an old worker excited for another thirty years, if we're smart and lucky.

(*Note to self: Don't ever start another business with $500 and a head full of ideas.*)

Thanks to you, good people, for picking up and wandering through this second book by Tsunami Press. If in some ways it might be said that we have spent over twenty-five years prepping for this moment, it stands that this is a good moment for a retrospective; an excellent moment to look back at some of the Bookstore Clerks, writers all, and Significant Others, who gave and still give good reason to hang in there, a Community of people in love with writing and the book.

What better way to tell the story of these people but through their own writing, generously given, written and re-written into a gift to receive with great pleasure and meaning and surprise.

I know nothing about anthologies, only that I always enjoy the ones I read. Fortunately, Steve has experience in building one right, and the ambition to build them one after another, which we intend to do, along with all the other books we look to have fun publishing. The idea that, as a new press, here is the moment for an anthology, to remember and honor the people who have done the work, and been the inspiration. That and twenty-seven years of daily work at Tsunami Books are what we have to offer.

A few words about the contributors to this anthology. . . I know them, many of them for twenty-plus years. There are personal reasons I wanted each of them to contribute. They are, every one, published authors, except for Emily, who has done whole books of illustrations, and my old partner Dave, who until recently has been too busy with the small glories of life to write, and me, also too busy, not to write, but to publish. I think you will enjoy everybody's work: competent, friendly Bookstore Clerks; understanding, caring Significant Others. Builders of Tsunami.

For now, if you would, please spend a moment with my own version of a contributors page, which Kawabata might consider "palm-of-the-hand stories."

Emily Poole: Seven years now in the Bookstore. An artist of merit and ethics, a true friend at work. At least a hundred people have asked if the original artwork for the cover of this book is for sale. But she gave it to Tsunami, where it sits near the counter on the top shelf of a set of shelves built with reclaimed wood by James Cramer to last a thousand years.

David Rhodes: Founder of Tsunami Books. "In it for the glory." A jazz-bo and a Joycean, with an exceptionally wise cool. We worked the counter together for twelve years. Made no money, well worth the effort.

Jenny Root: Tsunami's first full-time clerk, in the previous millennium. Forty hours per week, $9 per hour, at the time more than Dave and I made, combined. An invaluable worker, the stories, oh the stories. Her old dog, Shana, half wolf, slept peacefully by the counter, except for that time she bit the one guy who deserved it.

Dorianne Laux: She pumped gas to put herself through Mills, loves watching young poets work. She was here for more public reads than any of the profs.

Joseph Millar: A smiling, manly, working-class poet always thankful to be alive. Grew the best backyard crop of potatoes ever in South Eugene.

Matthew Dickman: A native of Portlandia with a happy face and gentle demeanor. A great, still-young poet, and now a writer of short stories. A twin, acolytes of Ginsberg and Levine. I hired him, not his dear brother, because he knew what work is. Lasted a week, the friendship forever.

Kelsey Yoder: The grad student all the other master's students of Creative Writing turned to for excitement and direction. She borrowed Alyssa Ogi's high-end cell phone to video Billy Strings, solo, on the Tsunami Stage. From Good Hope, Illinois, just up the road from where I grew up, in Mt. Sterling. After leaving Oregon, she applied for work at a little Bookstore in Colorado. The owner called for reference; turns out she and I may have been briefly married during recess one day in second grade.

Michael McGriff: A big, strong, sensitive young man from Coos Bay, who was either laughing hard or moping to Miles Davis over some short-term love just ended. One of the best of the poets, as big men need be, who studied the cover of every book he touched.

Maxine Scates: A straightforward thinker, a poet and gardener who digs deep. A well-loved and respected teacher of poetry. Has shared the Tsunami Stage often over twenty-seven years.

Meli Hull: She loved customer service; would run down the aisle to check stock. Walked to work every day for five years. When she and I were alone, we would both talk to ourselves. She dodged a bad-boy's knife behind the counter one day rather than give him the money.

Ken Babbs: We met just before Kesey died. He still brings us fresh milk from their cow every week. We talk books, we trade books and stories. We collaborate often, and we created something fun—Tsunami Press—may it outlive us both.

Eve Müller: Ann and Erik's daughter. Looks exactly like Erik, looks exactly like Ann. She took care of her father through his final months; read her excerpted hospice notes at Erik's memorial, at the Bookstore, the only Event through the Pandemic, the room full of tear-soaked masks.

Erik Muller: A lover and supporter of Oregon poets and Book-stores, a kind, funny man of deep honesty. There would be no Tsunami without Erik. The day in 2005 when Dave and I made known we were closing, belly-up, defeated, he and Ann came in from their daily walk through the Masonic Cemetery with a check-book. And here we are.

Carter McKenzie: She became a shareholder when that's what it took. She still comes to the meetings. A deeply principled human, a poet whose book *Naming Departure* kept me open though my own worst personal disaster.

Tom Titus: A fifth generation Oregonian, a PhD biologist, he loves to come to the Bookstore and talk. And we love to listen. Had his sixtieth birthday at Tsunami, a homemade blackberry pie and wine fest, the only time in store history all three toilets backed up.

Jorah LaFleur: For ten years the Maven of the monthly Eugene All-Ages Poetry Tslam at Tsunami. No one better to host the best slam poets in America, Jorah stepped up on the Tsunami Tstage over 2,000 times. And every time she "threw something down" it would be good to pick up.

Nina Kiriki Hoffman: Has attended close to a thousand science fiction writers' workshops at Tsunami. A Nebula winner, a universally revered Bookstore Clerk from another store, Nina, a shareholder, has come to our business meetings for eighteen years.

Bob Craven: Bob played his banjo almost as much as he worked on his PhD in American working-class poetry. A loyal, loving husband and father, the first in his Pennsylvania coal-mining family to go to college, there was something whimsical in the way he dusted the shelves.

Cecelia Hagen: For twenty years, the bright smooth boulder in the river of poets who showed up for the Monday night workshop. Had keys to the building. Maybe still does.

Valerie Ihsan: Managed the counter through the COVID; put on a double mask and got up close. She always did more than seemed possible. A lively, forgiving person with whom it is easy to be confidential, particularly in a Bookstore.

Brian Cutean: QTN. Shows up often, and does whatever, and it's always good. The only musician to have performed thirty-six consecutive years at the Oregon Country Fair. Has paid $150 per month for twenty years to live in a 150-square-foot cabin on the top of the hill on the edge of town.

Bronwynn Dean: She brought a frank, fun-loving intelligence every day to the job. A single mother of three, if there is a heaven, it emulates the love she has for her youngest.

Mose Tuzik Mosely: He only clerked about a week, and missed a couple of scheduled days. But how could you not love Mose, who took care of his dad, with honor and love, till the day he died.

Deb Casey: Even at her most serious, there appears a reasoned happiness. Has been to all our meetings. May she live forever in a handmade house full of books with John.

John Witte: For twenty-seven years a supporter, twenty of those years as managing editor of the *Northwest Review*. Exceptionally quiet, and grateful, a tall, thin, strong man. May he live forever in a handmade house full of books with Deb.

Steve Ellerhoff: Dr. Steve, a homecoming king and valedictorian from Des Moines with a PhD in English from Trinity in Dublin. Loves hilarity; both extremely accurate and forgiving. Proud to be a nerd. Forty-three-years old, one cavity, no sense of smell. Everyone wants to work next to Steve.

Elly Bookman: She kept dropping by, reapplying for the job, each time asking, "Did I tell you my name is Bookman?" Maybe the best listener of us all. What a genuine smile.

Scott Landfield: Grows figs and flowers, peas and tomatoes by the entrance to the Bookstore, which he built, with Chris, with salvaged wood and used books. Self-made, hard-working, fumbling, broke.

Thanks to the twenty-eight contributors—twenty-seven writers and one illustrator, fourteen Tsunami Clerks and fourteen Significant

Others. This is the moment for an anthology, to remember and honor the people who have done the work and been the inspiration through twenty-seven years of daily work at Tsunami Books.

Thanks, Folks,
Scott, Tsunami
Eugene, OR

THE SECRET BOOKSHOP

D.S. Rhodes

Three days out from Bend and nearing my destination. The wagon shifts beneath me as Winnie clip-clops through the pale afternoon light. Used to be a two-hour drive in the old days. Now it's a four-day jostle along the old highway to Burns. I take my time. There's no hurry, other than wanting to get home to The Bunker.

Bend turned out to be a waste of time. A *dangerous* waste of time. There were no books to be had. And just as I struck the road out of town I was searched by a gang of Proud Americans. Eight of them with shaved heads, full beards, and rather new-looking hardware. Only one of those Militia Boys appeared to be older than twenty. That was their leader.

He stood by while the junior squad went over my cart once and then again, seeking contraband. That is to say, books.

Fortunately, my books are hidden far too ingeniously for those amateurs to find. My cart—a sort of gypsy wagon that looks to be from some bygone era, but built ten years ago by my friend Sunny—has a false bottom under which I can fit something like a hundred books. Not that I've come up with a hundred books at one time since the crackdown. Books became mighty scarce after the Insurrection in '28, when the Proud Americans and Vow Holders and Bungalow Boys started calling the shots.

Right after that they started confiscating all the books deemed "unholy" by their synod over in Salem, which amounted to anything besides the Bible and the works of Billy Graham (though I heard that later there was some controversy about the Graham books, that they ended up in the fires, too). Nowadays—twenty years down the road—there are no more books in circulation. The bookstores were put to the torch and their proprietors sent to "re-education camps." Books mean knowledge and knowledge is power, two things the Militias and their backers can't allow to be spread around. Socrates was executed for far less.

Leaving Bend that way put a chill in me.

I'd found a small cache of books outside of Sisters at the home of an eccentric old widow. She had them well hidden, but the local paramilitaries had put the fear of God in her, and she'd gotten word to us of her desire to sell.

Like most folks, she'd given up the bulk of her books to the mobs of the Righteous and their book burnings. But her choicest volumes she kept hidden.

Sitting in her cabin overlooking the Metolius River, I sipped tea as she unearthed the books one by one from their hiding places. Five were buried in her backyard, in five different holes. The others were under the house, also under a foot of dirt. All were wrapped in plastic garbage bags.

"Raymond," she said, not looking up from her digging beneath the floorboards, "these books are my only family now. I hate to give them up. But I think those Militia Boys are getting desperate. I hear they're not finding many books these days." She handed me the last of them. "They'll be safer with you all. They need a new home. They need to be read. What good are they buried in dirt? Dead, they are."

Thus, I acquired slightly musty hardback copies—dust jackets intact—of *Mrs. Dalloway*, *Little Women*, *Gulliver's Travels*, *The Old Man and the Sea*, and poetry collections by Emily Dickinson and T.S. Eliot, plus a handful of paperbacks.

She kept her Bible prominently displayed on her coffee table, so the Militia Boys could see she's all right by them. And to have something to read.

Back in '28, when the government fell, things changed fast. Muslims were rounded up into massive internment camps out by La Grande and Ontario, under the pretext that they posed a terrorist threat. Actually, Christian Arabs too, the distinction being too fine for the junta. Many Jews ended up in the same camps. *"All the Semites in one basket!"* was a popular refrain at the time. Most Hispanics—US citizens or not—were simply dumped across the border with Mexico. African Americans faced a grimmer fate: in many places, the return of slavery. The Paramilitaries didn't call it slavery. It was "mandatory full employment." The people who didn't submit were locked up in privately operated prisons. Those who resisted—who took up arms and fought back—were quickly eliminated.

Not that there aren't still pockets of resistance in the mountains and deserts and other wild places—including some of the larger cities—still to this day. The Militias could never find them all. I run into them at times. Even do business with them. Two years ago I traded a load of hay to a real primitive outfit south of Mount Hood for a copy of Fukuoka's *One-Straw Revolution.* Alas, the resisters are a sorry few. At least they're living outside the Yoke, and that's something. If our endeavor is ever uncovered, I may find a place with one of these bands.

Before Sisters, I'd been travelling in the Willamette Valley. Just following my nose, as usual. Over by Springfield I passed on a collection of *Reader's Digest* and *National Geographic.* Maybe not outright contraband, but space is limited—both in my cart and back at The Bunker—and I'll be damned if I'm going to risk my neck for that sort of pulp.

At one time, Eugene was a hotbed of resistance to the New Regime. That was short-lived. This time through it looked like a bombed-out war zone. The surviving resisters headed for the hills. Those left in town are living in squalid camps of tents and tin. The nicer houses—the ones still standing, that is—are filled with the Righteous . . . and the wealthy.

Eugene and Corvallis and other clusters of resistance—mostly former college towns—are too dangerous to do business in anyway.

I tend to avoid them and stick to the margins. Needless to say, the colleges and universities were dismantled or reorganized.

Just to give an idea of the extent of the War on Books: an elderly lady living in a shack on the outskirts of Albany—she was apparently a doctor at one time—had used an old copy of *Gray's Anatomy* to insulate her walls and plug up the gaps that were making her place too drafty in the winter. The rest of the book she put into her outhouse for tissue.

Eventually the Militia Boys caught wind of this and came to her place and burned it to the ground—with her inside.

The State News reported that the militias had been forced to adopt a Zero Tolerance policy toward those harboring "unauthorized" books in their effort to stamp out terrorism, subversion and heresy.

I set out on this last scouting run over two months ago. I enjoy the slow pace, with my horse and cart. It's a little nerve-racking when the occasional car or truck goes screaming by. I try to travel back roads and stay well over to the side on the main ones. I've heard of other carts—even walkers—being run down by heedless drivers.

There aren't many automobiles left in the hands of private citizens—and gas is even more scarce. But the militias and the police and the "National Guard" (now in the hands of the Vow Holders) still have access to motor vehicles *and* fuel. So it's mostly them I see speeding by. On their way to some urgent business.

My cart, besides being where I live when on the road, doubles as a farm wagon. I'm always sure to have produce on board: squash, or beans in sacks; corn; sometimes tomatoes. Anything that will deter a thorough search of the wagon. I often have a load of hay as well. Every rancher recognizes the need for hay, so they generally wave me through the roadblocks.

As I was saying, I hit the road at the end of August, after the annual ten weeks of scorching 100+ weather abated some. During the Heat, there's not much moving about. I like to stay at The

Bunker—that's the common name of the bookshop. It's also known as The Cave, The Shelter, The Sanctuary, and many other things. Nice and cool in The Bunker. I get a lot of reading done during the Heat.

I don't think the place has any proper name. Sylvia and Ernie—the proprietors—like it that way. Underground and out of sight.

Literally. The bookstore occupies an old Cold War fallout shelter from the early '60s—Cuban Missile Crisis vintage. Sylvia and Ernie bought the ranch house and the hundred acres it sits on back in the mid-2020s—seeing what was coming—and started repurposing it as an underground bookstore. They added on, dug new rooms, and now it's a network of sprawling caves, room after glorious room, filled floor-to-low-ceiling with books. Practically invisible from the surface, it looks like an abandoned ruin. Solar panels embedded at ground level provide all the lighting and other electrical needs. Behind the bookshop we hollowed out rooms for living spaces and a shared kitchen where the three of us make meals, eat and sleep.

Visitors park their vehicles in the dilapidated barn outside. Motorcycles, bicycles, horses and carts, some automobiles or trucks (mostly bio-diesel monstrosities). It's a fragile balance Sylvia and Ernie have struck between customers knowing about the place and still keeping it secret. They've developed a process by which new customers are recommended by existing customers, with background checks and the like. It's not ideal, but they've managed to stay in business all these years without mishap. Business is brisk enough to stay alive, and discreet enough to stay undetected.

Sometimes the bookshop has the feel of a library or museum—or mausoleum. The books and walls absorb all sound, so there's a crypt-like hush as one wanders the many rooms. I don't know for sure, but I'd guess it's got to be the largest repository of books anywhere on the West Coast. Sylvia claims there are over a hundred thousand volumes.

The customers know to be inconspicuous, if not invisible. And to have a quick story ready at hand, in case they are stopped by the

Authorities, or by roving gangs of Militia Boys. Some claim to be mushroom hunters, or deer and elk hunters. Many just claim to be lost and ask directions—a plausible enough ruse in these wastelands. I suppose it would only take one frightened booklover, captured by the Militia Boys, to end our run. That sort of makes the end sound inevitable, and maybe it is. But we'll keep it going as long as we can.

After all, people *need* books.

Those folks that make it to The Bunker leave their ride in the barn and enter the collapsing ranch house. A set of rickety stairs leads to a dank basement, populated by rodents, spiders, sometimes snakes.

At the rear of the basement an unpainted door opens into the original fallout shelter, dug by the survivalist rancher and his wife. World War III never materialized, but at least it was a cool, dry place to store their canned goods and ammo. The first room of the shelter looks completely conventional: bunks for four, shelves of canned goods and closets for storage; an ancient generator helps clutter the room; a rough kitchen and a composting toilet behind a curtain tracked on the ceiling.

But go into the closet and you find a fairly well-hidden door. Behind that door one enters an entirely different realm: The Secret Bookshop. Climate-controlled for optimum temperature and humidity, track lighting along the shelves to provide the minimum amount of light a person would need to browse comfortably, sensors bringing the light up and down automatically as needed. At the very back are the private quarters, with a real kitchen and bathroom. The water comes from the old well, pumped underground to our hidden lair.

It's a good life. And, as Sylvia always adds, it's a mission too.

Purchases are limited to ten books at a time, to minimize suspicion if patrons run into trouble. Customers pay with Old American Dollars, gold, silver, sometimes food or other bartered necessities. A guy came in one time with five boxes of toilet paper he traded for some old car manuals and permaculture books.

I set out after the Heat, my wagon loaded with hay, for the Valley. Now I'm headed home, a meager forty books aboard. Two months' effort for forty books. The militias aren't the only ones having trouble finding books these days.

But I am *so* looking forward to Sylvia's beans and rice and cornbread—and Ernie's homemade hooch. I've been out of spirits since Silverton.

Ever since the New Regime passed its Gun Laws—all adult males are required to carry at least one firearm at all times—I've hauled along an ancient, but functioning, Colt .45. I even learned to shoot the thing as part of my disguise. Hopefully I'll never have to use it, though it does come in handy as intimidation. Also, it's the perfect prop, the kind of sidearm that elicits wonder and admiration when the Militia Boys stop me to check if I'm carrying. Am I ever.

So now, after this long road, and over two months, I'm approaching The Bunker. No one on the road for miles and miles in either direction. I take a left turn onto what was once Rattlesnake Road, a paved two-laner that shoots straight north for a couple miles before a climb and weave through some rolling hills, dead brown this time of year except for the pale green of the sagebrush.

A lovely smell rises from the land. Emptiness. Not even cattle anymore. Just plain emptiness as far as the eye can see. And blessed silence. The silence that allows you to hear the sound of the wind in the sage and dead grasses. Occasional chips and chirps from the brush. The patter of a jackrabbit. Oh, this land is full of life, if you know where to look. Fortunately, most people don't.

Things out here know how to hide, so we feel right at home. Though I suppose every critter on or under the ground has its hawk or coyote that will one day make a meal of it.

That's a disconcerting thought.

I pick up my pace.

From the next rise I see the ranch house, so weathered it blends right into the surrounding landscape. The road is rutted and potholed. A desolate place. Still, I see tracks leading to the ranch. Car tires. Horseshoe prints. Wagon ruts like those my cart leaves. That can't be helped. We make a point of regularly sweeping away tracks that come near the ranch. But right now, looking over the tableau below me—dilapidated ranch house, collapsing barn, rotted fence timbers—it's hard to imagine anyone giving this place more than a cursory glance.

Unless they're on the run, looking for a place to hide.

Sylvia and Ernie have taken in a few fugitives and refugees over the years, though never for long, and always after a thorough vetting process to insure they posed no threat to the shop's invisibility.

I'm thinking about the last such fugitive, back in the spring. Rufus. A red-headed, green-eyed tweaker, talking a mile a minute. Keyed-up and definitely on *something*, though who knows what these days.

This Rufus came poking around the ranch house, thinking to hole up there for a while, until whatever heat was after him had lost interest, or lost his trail.

The Bunker has sensors in the house, of course, and we knew he was there. So Ernie and I went up and had a talk with him. Well, Ernie did the talking. I just stood behind him with the Colt loosely in my hand—not loaded, but damn intimidating.

Rufus nearly jumped out of his skin when we suddenly appeared from nowhere.

"Hey, Mister, hey! Don't shoot, man. I'm cool!"

Now, Ernie is a quality hombre and a true humanitarian. He's also a damn fine judge of character, and he quickly assessed the situation.

"What's your name, son?"

The redheaded stranger stared goggle-eyed at us for a minute. I thought maybe he'd swallowed his tongue.

But then he said, "Name's Rufus. I'm cool. Don't shoot!"

"Not gonna shoot you, son. Just want to know what you're doing here. And where you're headed. And who's after you."

That brought Rufus up short a moment. Then he launched back into his speed-jabber.

"Nobody after *me*, man. I mean not nobody. Just not somebody, you know?"

Ernie raised his eyebrows but said nothing.

Rufus took a breath and went on. "It's the County Boys. Sheriff and such. They don't amount to much, right? Couldn't find their way out of a twenty-dollar whorehouse. You know what I mean? Just saw this here abandoned old place. Thought I'd hunker down for a few days. Didn't mean nothin' by it. Just layin' low, see? Didn't know it was already occupied, like . . ."

Ernie held up his hand to stop the word-flow.

"Nobody told you about this place? You just stumbled on it? Is that right?"

"Yes, sir, that's right. Just cruisin' by and saw it. Thought, there's my place . . ."

Ernie cut in again and said slowly, "What are they after you for, Rufus?"

"Well, it's like this, see . . . I busted out the county slam in Salem. Hitched and walked all the way out here lookin' for someplace just like this—abandoned and such . . ."

"What were you in for, son?"

"Oh, this and that. Mostly being a nuisance to society. And knockin' over a 7-Eleven in Lebanon about three years back."

There was a long silence then.

Ernie is a large man. Large in body and larger in presence. He towered over Rufus. Loomed over him.

He said flatly, though not unkindly, "Rufus, you can't stay here. I'm sorry but you've got to move on."

Rufus' face registered angry defiance, but he was overmatched. Ernie was a force to be reckoned with. And I still held the Colt.

Ernie said, "Wait here," and vanished into the cellar.

So I stood in the dark of that abandoned ranch house with Rufus. I could hear him grinding his teeth, but he didn't dare try anything.

Neither of us said a word.

Moments later, Ernie reappeared from below with a package of food and a couple of Zane Grey paperbacks. Rufus took these without a word and we watched him exit by the front door and move away northward, down the cracked and disintegrating road, just as the sun went down behind the western horizon.

"Good riddance," I said in the dark house.

"Let's hope so," was all Ernie said back.

I don't know why I'm thinking of Rufus as I approach The Bunker. But I am.

I drive Winnie into the barn and see an old beater BMW motorcycle, an ancient corn-burner Toyota station wagon, and another horse-drawn farm cart, an open flatbed type. The horse stands stoically munching hay in one of the stalls, next to Sylvia and Ernie's twin mares. Winnie joins them with a contented snort.

It's a real process to extricate my stash of books from the cart, so I decide I'll come back and do it after checking in with Sylvia and Ernie, having a bite to eat, and cleaning up. Out of habit, I look up and down the drive, then up into the sky before I sidle through the front door, down the basement stairs and into the fallout shelter.

Entering the bookshop, I sense tension in the air.

One of the customers whose vehicle I'd seen in the barn—from the looks of him I'm guessing the Toyota—nearly runs right into me on his way out. He seems in an unnatural hurry, and when he does see me he lets out a reflexive yelp of surprise. He carries a small backpack, which I can tell is stuffed with books.

"Excuse me," he says brusquely.

I shift and he shimmies past, out the door into the fallout shelter. His behavior isn't unheard of. Our customers are often a bit jumpy. After all, buying and concealing books is a capital offense. But this fellow sets me on edge.

Then I see Sylvia loading a pair of motorcycle bags with what look like some thirty building and gardening books, and I can tell something isn't right. The motorcycle guy darts past me to the exit and I'm left facing Sylvia.

Without a word she comes over and grabs me in a fierce hug, nearly knocking me off my feet.

"Oh, Ray," she says. And that's all she says.

Ernie comes bustling in then and says in a flat, matter-of-fact voice, "Oh, good. You're here. Doris just got here about a half hour ago. She says the jig is up. We've been discovered, Raymond. We've finally been discovered. The State Militia is on its way."

Ernie seems weirdly detached. By his watery eyes I can tell he's had a few shots of the hooch.

Despair wells up from deep inside me. A sadness beyond words. Ernie grabs my arm and pulls me forcefully down the length of the bookshop to our living quarters. Sylvia follows. In our kitchen we meet up with Doris. The two women embrace, but both are dry-eyed. Tough women.

Doris is another book hunter, from down around Takilma. Unlike me, she works freelance, and has for many years, moving books from here to there, wherever they are needed. A stout woman, powerfully built, she stands only five-foot-four. She wears a straw cowboy hat and large belt buckle and plays the part of rancher or rancher's wife quite convincingly, though she is neither.

Doris plays the role so well that she moves effortlessly through the circles of the various authorities and militias. She keeps tabs on them for the book networks. She's able to act as a lookout, and to move books around right under their noses.

Sylvia and Doris—seeing Ernie and me paralyzed and lost in a maze of disbelief, denial and grief—take charge of the situation.

"Come on, Ernie," Sylvia says quietly but firmly. "It's time for Operation Spadefoot. Let's get to it."

Ernie nods once and passes through to their bedroom, clicking on a light and stumbling around in a daze. I go into my own room and grab my bug-out pack with clothes, food, water and gear for a week or more.

Sylvia stands in the outer apartment and gives calm, quiet orders.

"Doris. You and Ray take whatever you want—whatever you can carry—and get a move on. Doris, you'll be heading south. Ray you should probably take Rattlesnake north."

We've talked about this moment for years, but now it has arrived, the sense of unreality is overpowering.

Doris and I go to the collectibles cabinet to grab what we can. I carefully pull out a handful of first printings that I've meditated on for years, imagining this scenario: *Siddhartha*, *Gravity's Rainbow*, *Shikasta*, *The Telling*, *The Man in the High Tower*, *Fahrenheit 451*, Huxley's *Island*, and a gorgeous collection of William Blake poems. At the last moment I pick up a copy of *Parnassus on Wheels* and hand it to Doris with an ironic smile.

Doris goes for more spiritual, metaphysical authors: Thich Nhat Hanh, Alan Watts, Pema Chödrön, Eckhart Tolle, Hazrat Inayat Khan, Ram Dass. She also takes some Toni Morrison and Barbara Kingsolver for fiction.

It feels strange removing the books from their sacred abode. I'm conscious of just how priceless they have become. But I also know what happens next—what Operation Spadefoot means. The Great Basin Spadefoot is a toad that burrows in the ground and can go dormant for years if need be. I've been living in this expanded fallout shelter for eighteen years and was Ernie's partner in planting the dynamite in the ranch house.

The four of us bustle up and out of The Secret Bookshop, the men stumbling and cursing, the women businesslike.

In the barn there is a breaker box, and in it one 30-watt breaker labeled only with a large red exclamation point. While Doris and I work on stashing our rescued books in our carts, Ernie and Sylvia walk to the breaker box.

They place both of their hands on the red exclamation-point breaker, together.

Without a word, they flip it.

The ground shakes.

Pieces of the house pelt the sides and roof of the barn.

The Secret Bookshop—refuge of so many volumes; so many words; so many ideas—is buried beneath the demolished rubble of a nondescript ranch house on the high desert plateau, somewhere between Bend and Burns.

It lies buried there, and will remain so until someone digs it out. An archaeologist of some future age, perhaps. Or a treasure hunter. Hopefully not one of the militant book-burning groups. But maybe it'll be us—Ernie and Sylvia and me—once this wave of insanity and terror has run its course and passed on, as it certainly will.

Doris says the Militia Boys will be here by this evening, so we best be moving along.

Ernie and Sylvia are heading north and east on horseback to stay with friends on the Snake River. Doris will drive her flatbed cart south towards her home in Takilma.

And I?

I'm going to reconnect with some resisters I know up in the Wallowas. People who know about sieges and paramilitary militias and forced relocations. Mostly Nez Perce, and those of us refugees they've allowed to join them.

A great dust cloud rises from the demo'd ranch house. I wonder what the Militia Boys will make of that. It's hard to imagine them digging all the way through that wreckage to find the caves underneath. But who knows? We had one chance to protect the mother lode and we took it.

We all four say our good-byes once more. No tears, and no fear either.

Resignation, I would call it. Maybe, eventually, even acceptance.

We head off in our three directions, not even bothering with the tracks anymore.

So now I'm back on the road again, for a while. Time to get under cover as soon as I can. The sun bakes the desert all around me, as crickets whirr and a few vultures circle above. A lazy sort of day. No sign of human existence but for the dust plumes behind me.

"Winnie," I say in the glaring silence. "Time is on our side. Nothing lasts. But all things eventually return. And that feels about right. Time is on *our* side."

Jenny Root

RENASCENT

With a name like Root, shall I begin with the roux? A recipe rife with ritual, a rendering rich and strange. Aye, at heart I'm ruddy as a rainbow, a rouged ragout of wry delight. A riot on the dance floor, but a wreck in the middle of the night. You see, I've a wretched reputation, a runway of past regrets. I've rummaged reefer, rented rooms by the hour, rehearsed reverse roulette. Still, I wrestle the ratfinks with my ruthless repartee. The roadshow I remember—a reel among the ruffians, my rivals laid to ruin. With Romeo after Romeo I rode my inner rodeo—a rendezvous, a revelry—remorse riding herd. One ran away. One reaped the gun. For one, revenge took a savage turn and I lost all that I'd won. He wrung my rogue heart until I heard my own name run. I wept for the ransom; rue it hasn't come. Razored, my resistance, my rime of rote replies. Now I ration reprisals, readjust as scenes require. My rehab a raging river, my rifle a rook in disguise.

THAT WHICH LIES BESIDE THE SLOUGH

> "('Let us now go even unto Bethlehem, and see this
> thing which is come to pass.'). Occasionally *which*
> seems preferable to *that* . . ." — *The Elements of Style*

The cigarettes that once touched their lips lie smoldering
      beside the slough.
The cigarettes, which once were whole as children, lay crushed
      into the mud beside the slough.

The blankets that lay heaped beneath the bridge covered them
      head to toe.
The blankets, which once lay folded upon a quiet shelf, trembled in
      the scolding wind.

The dog that nosed the blankets as it passed wasn't allowed to
      linger.
The dog, which pulled back on its leash to linger, smelled
      something curious, so curious.

The people who walked the dog tried offering privacy to the
      blankets.
The people who walked the dog thought privacy a kindness to the
      blankets, which trembled in the testifying wind.

The storm that took the town by surprise had everyone fooled.
The storm, which shook the town by the throat, snapped trees in
      its gnashing teeth.

The storm that raised the water in the slough howled like Gabriel.
The storm, which howled like an angel on fire, raised the water,
          aroused the water in the drunken slough.

The sweatshirt that once lay crumpled in the weeds was pulled in
          and sucked by the dirty lips of the slough.
The sweatshirt, red and torn, which has known the shape of
          woman, swirled a scarlet torch song upon the wreck of
          slough.

The people who had seen the sweatshirt for weeks were glad of its
          riddance.
The people, whom the shirt had seen from its bed in the crumpled
          weeds, wondered where all the debris had gone from
          beside the slough, beneath the bridge.

The song that rose from the wrack held a rose for the morning air.
The song, rose and risen, which hovered in the air like smoke,
          ushered the greeting dog away, away.

ECLIPSE AND FIRE

One week before she died we watched the sun
erased, our light, our warmth, even our shadows

canceled, disappeared, though surely they
hadn't left, were merely absent, would

return to us, anchor us to earth, home
spinning among stars; even with this tumor

resurrected without our knowing, she
walked wherever we went, her age, her pace

guiding us from lakeshore to gravel bar
back to camp near a wilderness on fire:

grey smoke eating our horizon as we
grinned for the camera, then stared, stunned:

the moon a portal, our dog dying, our bodies
shivering with life, this life, oh life.

Dorianne Laux

DRIVING THROUGH
THE AVENUE OF THE GIANTS
VIA THE TRINITY RIVER BYWAY

A flitch of sawn redwood for sale by the roadside,
the crosscut revealing its rings, maybe one hundred,
showing off its newness on the earth. The flitch
has no eyes, only a flat ceiling of amber lumber,
and because it's dead, no more longing or hunger
for its brothers, the roots of its sisters, the honeyed
breath of its mother. It now belongs to some human
in boots and sunscreen, hauling it off to a red truck
filled with nuts and bolts, a case of booze.
It will now reside in a glassed-in living room, collecting
dust, someone's feet balanced on its rim, watching
the Novocain of a commercial on TV. Such trespass
occurs daily, common as river water lapping up
on the swash of sand and pebbles growing even
smaller than they already are, until you and I
are becoming air, wary of the nothing
we came from, watchful of the nowhere
we can go.

REDWOODS

The first time I entered a forest
I saw the trees, of course, huddled
together in rings, thin veils of mist
between their branches, some dead
but still standing, or fallen thigh bones
on the desiccated floor, but I also saw
the great buttery platters of fungus
climbing like stepping stones
up their shaggy trunks: *tzadee, tzadee,*
tzadee, each a different size: small
to large or large to small, as if some
rogue architect had been cocky enough
to install them on the stunned trees'
northern sides, leading up to the balconies
of their one-ton boughs. I was here
to investigate my place among them,
these giants, 3,000 years old, still
here, living in my lifetime. I should
have felt small, a mere human—petty
in my clumsy boots, burrs in my socks
while these trees held a glossary of stars
in their crowns, their heads up there
in the croissant-shaped clouds,
the wisdom of the ages flowing up
through from root to branchlet—
though rather, I felt large
inside my life, the sum of Jung's
archetypes: the self, the shadow,
the anima, the persona of my
personhood fully recognized

and finally accepted, the nugget
of my being, my shadow
of plush light. I felt like I was
climbing up those fungal discs
toward something endless, beyond
my birth and death, into my here-ness
and now-ness, the scent and silence
overwhelming me, seeping back
into my pores. You had to have
been there, my limbs tingling,
ancient, mute.

UNDERSTORIES

You can gather enough stones to build
a chimney or a pyramid, the only difference
is how many and time, 200 or 2 million,
one day or 20 years, the difference between
necessary and epic, a small miracle
or a serious marvel.

You can dig out a backyard pond
or a Suez Canal. One loves ducks, the other
is a reservoir of death, 120,000 men, 200,000
sheep and cows. A safe harbor or a murder site.

Today I'm trying to love the beauty
of a cathedral, its struts and buttresses,
the elegance of the orange twin cables
swaying above the Golden Gate, ripples
glittering below. Fingers dipped
into a bowl of holy water.
But I cannot be fully seduced.
There's no place left in me
that hasn't been pierced. All I can see
is the unskilled workers who dug out
the foundations, the glaziers and masons,
ten wedging one granite slab
above another, anonymous under the sun,
grit and sweat lacing their foreheads.
Or a man hanging upside down
painting a steel beam, scratching his
name between two rivets with a nail.

Joseph Millar

ART MUSEUM

You've just left the glass mansion of art
with its roof beam reaching to paradise
and its sills sunk into the rock of the earth:
limestone and quartz, granite, basalt.
Its wine glass and tapestry,
fractures and planes, its suffering,
thorns and blood.

The city has risen behind you chalk-white,
its darkness brushing your eyes,
electric trolleys and wind off the bay,
chambers of blossoms and yellow leaves
hanging in lit clusters over the tracks,
over the Filbert Street steps.
Maybe you'll live to a hundred and ten
climbing them twice a day
with your water bottle and sunflower seeds
trying to invent some flagrant language,
spendthrift and primitive, harsh.

Sometimes we think
we have done everything
but we have not done everything.

If you want to get any writing done,
ride the Number Five going west
to a small house on Fulton Street.
You should go inside and stare at the wall
on a late March day after work

letting a fly crawl over your knuckles
and using ink blackened
with soot from the stove
where you cooked the zucchini
and scrambled eggs,
where the dog lies down, the links
of his collar shining deep in his fur,
near where the dark red women
make music, not thinking about tomorrow:
Nina Simone in a yellow turban
singing in smoky French,
or Joan Armatrading
with her casket guitar
looking out over the park

and watching the ducks quarrel in the mud,
the tramp's raw hands
sticking out from his coat sleeves,
the chess players bent to their plans,
the same ancient faces hanging there
restless, agitated, waiting for dusk
or waiting for summer
to arrive from the south
with its fat leaves and bird's nests,
its earthworms and pollen,
its gold hair smelling
of beeswax, its angels of tall grass,
its wide open fields,
slow tides and rhythms,
and waking up early,
its birds that whistle and sing.

ANTOINETTE

It was a perilous holiday season
waiting for you to finish your shift
on Jones Street in the City,
in the ticket window of Alex de Renzy's
Triple-X Screening Room.
You would slide out the door
in canvas shoes and a raincoat
like a lost saint
in a Graham Greene novel,
distant and abandoned,
riding the transit bus
back to the El Rey Apartments,
saint of dark eyes and pill bottles,
of somnambulist sex in high-ceilinged rooms
with their avocado plants
and quaalude balcony
high in the trees over San Rafael
and facing away from the street
in the days before Christmas '74,
each of us entirely alone
numbly holding onto each other
till we could disappear into sleep.

CHAPTER 13

Hung behind glass with its brushed copper frame
in the bankruptcy lawyer's office
high above Van Ness Avenue
a giant photo of Rimbaud's face,
with its shocked freckles and narrow eyes
staring venomously down at the chair
where I wait for my attorney
to return from lunch.
I have eighteen hundreds to get him started,
no checks, no credit,
holding a huge file of collection notices,
which he scans briefly,
removing his blue sharkskin jacket
and looking sleepily down.

I can hear the March wind outside
making creaky metallic sounds
like a tow truck preparing to hook up my car,
I imagine the snows of my grandmother's shame
settling deeply up to my waist. The lawyer
looks up through designer lenses
and a night-moth
rustles the window shade:
maybe the ghost of Rimbaud the profligate
waking up in the grass of a ditch,
on a whorehouse couch
or a tramp steamer,
throwing his arms open, lifting his face
trying to swallow the light.

LEVELING UP

Matthew Dickman

I am death, Death thinks.

Then worries that he thought it too loud. Or accidentally said it out loud so that the kid in the green denim jacket and Whitesnake T-shirt might have heard him. But he didn't. He just thought it and the thought bloomed right there in the front of his skull like a lilac tree in the middle of a dry and cracked riverbed. The night sky moving above the riverbed and the stars and the dumb moon hanging out in the dark with its dumb mouth open.

I am death, Death thinks. I was in Carthage. I was in Salem. I was in Poland, Germany, Mississippi. I was in the Athens, Antonine, Cyprian, Justinian, all of them, all the plagues. I was in London riding on the backs of rats, all the rats. I have been in every variant of every virus fit for a pig. I was on that flight and that flight, on all those flights. I walked into the high school like it was a normal day. The high school, the elementary school, the kindergarten, the church, the nightclub, the mall, this very mall just a couple years ago. I aimed and fired. I created religion just by opening my eyes, by sneezing. Me taking a shit erects whole cathedrals, whole mosques, hundreds of temples dedicated to escaping me. I was in Rwanda, Congo, Biafra. I'm in every dumb-shit shoebox that every dumb-shit father has hidden under his bed, on the shelf in his closet, just waiting for his kids to come home and I'm fully-loaded, safety-off. I am threaded through everything. Every street, every organ, every minute. I'm in the water. I was in Pompeii, fucking Pompeii, and I can't get this stupid asshole on the screen to move fast enough not to get eaten by fucking ghosts. I've stood here for two hours and

MATTHEW DICKMAN

can't get past the level with the fucking pear. I just want to reach the banana level. I just want to win. But the universe is always like, *Hey, stay in your lane, dude. Just do what you're good at, do what you know*, says the universe. Pounding it into our heads with a hammer the very size of the universe until our heads are smashed on the concrete. Fucking universe with all its uptight ideas about balance and what comes around goes around.

The Ms. Pac-Man that Death has been pouring his whole afternoon into has just been eaten again. That's the third time this game. A rather short game. Death smacks the joystick and it bends all the way left then springs back up. A message appears on the screen: INSERT QUARTER TO CONTINUE GAME IN 10, 9, 8, 7, 6, 5, 4, 3, 2, 1 . . . GAME OVER, flashing.

Death is out of quarters. He is fifteen years old, whatever that means in death-years, dog-years, etc. He's wearing baggy jeans and a Powell Peralta T-shirt. The one with the skull and a snake between its teeth, a laurel wreath made out of lightning for a crown. Around Death's neck is a leather necklace and a small cross. He stares at the screen where a happy Ms. Pac-Man is busy running around avoiding ghosts and eating dots, eating cherries, eating strawberries, apples pretzels, fucking bananas. The words INSERT ONE QUARTER FOR ONE PLAYER / TWO QUARTERS FOR TWO PLAYERS blinking on the screen. He picks at the acne on his chin. He feels sweaty, no—sticky! That's what he feels. He feels sticky for no reason.

Death looks around. The arcade is full of other kids even though it's a Tuesday afternoon. All the tired threats teachers and parents make about truancy officers picking up wayward children and fining them, dragging them off to prison or marching them back to their high school by the elbow, by the ear, and right into the principal's office are bullshit. If you're not screaming your head off or walking through the food court naked or getting caught shoplifting, the security guards will leave you alone and the other adults, the ones shopping, walking aimlessly around, the ones stopping by the man near the escalators playing bad Chopin on a baby grand

26

piano, tapping their feet, nodding their heads, well—they won't even notice you. They have enough on their plates. None of them are going to stop you and say, *Hey, shouldn't you be in school?* The rare time that that does happen, it's often some guy in his thirties trying to flirt with a girl who's fifteen or sixteen or twelve. The way he says it like he's saying, *Hey, you and I are the same, you and I break the rules.* Super creepy. He doesn't even have a car. He took the bus here. Maybe two buses. Just hangs out at the mall all day looking for kids to talk to, to touch, to take away to some basement, some nearby empty studio with his no-car-having ass. Sometimes he finds someone whose eyes widen when he tells them he's a photographer. *You could definitely be a model,* he says. *You have an old soul,* he says, *I can see it in your eyes,* and if they listen, if they believe him, what they follow him towards is death. If he finds a lot of kids who will listen then the news media will give him a scary name, a catchy name, they'll call him something like The Mall Stalker or title a newspaper article something like Death Comes to The Mall.

But he's not death, Death thinks.

He's unbelievably average.

A pair of khaki pants and a windbreaker.

He's someone with a last name for Christ's sake.

A human being. Adult acne. A comb in his back pocket. A voice that sounds like its being squeezed out of a balloon.

You gonna stand there all day or you gonna play, dude?

What?

Death turns around and standing behind him is a girl his age wearing one of those vintage dresses Courtney Love wears, black combat boots, black jelly bracelets, her hair cut in a bob.

If you're not gonna play I'd like a turn, she says.

But she says this really slow, like Death is slow or something.

She says it like, IIIF . . . YOUUU . . . ARRRE . . . NOOOT . . . GOOONA . . . PLAAAY . . . III'D . . . LIIIKE . . . AAAH . . . TUUURN.

And then she smiles.

Of course. No. Yes. Yeah, it's all yours, whatever, says Death.

Death is flustered.

The girl smiles again. Then makes a frown. Then smiles.

I'm Jennifer, she says.

Okay, Death says.

I'm telling you, Jennifer says, because it seems like something you would want to ask me but are too shy or whatever, or like high or weird—or whatever—to ask yourself so I'm just getting it out of the way.

Pause.

Silence.

Death locked into a hundred-yard stare.

Sooooo? And you are?

I'm Anu, Death says.

What's-Who?

Anu. A-N-U. It's Egyptian or something.

Whoa, your parents were some kind of hippies, huh, Anu? Well, now that we know each other's names and we're friends and there's no stranger-danger how about you let me play, or we can play doubles?

Anu reaches into his jean pockets for a quarter. Nothing.

I've got you covered, Anu with the weird hippie name, Jennifer says, and pulls out a plastic Ziploc sandwich bag full of quarters from the oversized pockets she sewed onto her dress.

Anu and Jennifer go back and forth, taking turns moving Ms. Pac-Man around the grid, avoiding ghosts, eating a piece of fruit, then eating the ghosts themselves. Jennifer is talking about the Pixies and how fucked up and heartbreaking it was that Kim Deal left the band or got kicked out or whatever, but how could she not, I mean who could put up with someone like Frank Black and her sister in and out of rehab. But anyway, Jennifer continues, it's fine because Kim started her own band with her sister called the Breeders and their album *Last Splash* is so good, have you heard it? Do you know the track "Cannonball?" Oh I love how it starts with that bassline, it's so cool, if I could be in any band it would be in the

Breeders or L7 or Babes in Toyland or something where girls are kicking all kinds of ass. What about you, Anu, what band would you be in if you could be in any band?

Anu can't think of any band. It's like all the music he has ever listened to has disappeared. He can't even think of the words *the Beatles*. Well, he can, sort of, but he only sees actual beetles in his mind, crawling through the dirt. *Smashing* and *Pumpkins* float by but all he sees are some kids throwing an old couple's Jack-O-Lantern against a red front door. Dinosaur Jr. is just a young dinosaur walking through some tall grass, leaning down and chewing it in the field of his neocortex. He's looking at the Ms. Pac-Man Jennifer is now moving across the screen, chasing the now blinking ghosts but he is also looking at Jennifer. He can feel his armpits getting swampy. He can feel the acne on his chin, his forehead, sort of humming. Jennifer looks like someone who may or may not get her nose pierced when she's old enough. Her lip pierced. A tattoo. All around Jennifer, other kids are pushing buttons really fast, shooting down centipedes from outer space or aiming at zombies with bright red and blue guns, eating candy, drinking Pepsi and orange soda. Anu is looking at Jennifer's mouth, how her teeth glisten, the half-moon earrings she's wearing, one in each ear, and he feels something, some music, some memory, building up. A pressure like an underground volcano.

I am death, Anu thinks, c'mon I know this. I know I have a band I like.

Hello? Earth to Anu.

THE VIOLENT FEMMES!!! Anu yells.

Jennifer's eyes widen.

Right, okay, okay, she says. Don't spaz out, it's just a question. Yikes. I like the Violent Femmes too. "Blister in the Sun." So fucking good. I mean, I wouldn't go around the mall screaming about them but yeah, Anu with the hippie parents, you have good taste.

Jennifer's last Ms. Pac-Man gets eaten by a ghost and Anu starts his turn.

I saw them once, says Anu. I saw them open for Primus.

Great, now he can think of all the bands. In all the world. In all of time. But Anu doesn't say, Yeah, the Violent Femmes were rad but also I saw Jimi Hendrix at a party in a flat in London and once caught Mozart playing out when he was a kid, or, I sat in the room with Kurt Cobain the day he hummed a song he was working out in his mind right before he loaded his shotgun and blew the top of his head off. Sat there, humming along with him, making up lyrics that would never be written down.

It was a great show, Anu says, though the Femmes were so much better than Primus. They had the whole crowd going apeshit from the first song. Everyone moving like one big wave out in the ocean. When Primus came on it was like listening to the radio and it took like three songs for the mosh pit to get started.

That's cool, says Jennifer. Hey, what school do you go to?

What do you mean? says Anu.

What do you mean what do I mean? What school? What grade are you in?

Anu thinks about this.

Oh! Yeah. Right, he says, I'm homeschooled right now but that's not gonna be like forever or whatever. I think I'm probably starting regular school next year, um, sophomore year.

Homeschooled, huh? Jennifer looks at Anu's clothes, his hair. You don't look like one of those right-wing Christian or Mormon or whatever homeschooled kids. You look normal. You look like someone I would bump into in the hall.

Like you said, Anu says, my parents are hippies. It's less religious homeschooling and more eco-conscious stuff. Mother Earth stuff. I don't mind it. I have friends in the neighborhood and sometimes I get to spend the afternoon in the mall like today, and once I even spent the whole day exploring all around the ohfuckmeyoumotherfucker!

The blue ghost chomps his Ms. Pac-Man alive.

GAME OVER.

Jennifer looks at her plastic sandwich bag lying on the console next to her joystick.

Well, Anu, just one quarter left.

Jennifer looks up at the clock in the arcade. The hour hand is a fifties-looking spaceship and it's right at three o'clock while the second hand, which is an asteroid, goes flying near the top.

Tell you what, Jennifer says, you keep it. Play one more game. I have to go anyway. If I'm not home by 3:30 my folks will lose their minds.

Jennifer hands the bag with its one quarter to Anu and when she does, his index finger grazes her palm. It feels to Anu like the whole arcade stops, time stops, everything freezes. Jennifer right in the middle of it all, of his mind, saying something, the guy behind the prize counter counting pink ski-ball tickets, a kid about to drop a slice of pizza, someone aiming an old fashioned-looking rifle at a duck on a screen, all frozen but for Anu.

I am love, Anu thinks.

And then, just like a movie, everything speeds up again. The slice of pizza falls to the floor, the tickets are exchanged for a cheap knock-off Rubik's Cube, a duck gets shot, music plays and Jennifer is looking at Anu again.

You are definitely strange, says Jennifer, but I'm glad we met. I'd give you my number but something tells me you wouldn't know what to do with it.

Anu doesn't say anything but he does smile.

Alright, Anu of The Arcade, says Jennifer, I've got a quest for you. It's older than life itself. Are you ready to accept it?

Anu nods his head.

Jennifer takes the sandwich bag out of Anu's hand, removes the quarter and raises it up into the air.

You must defeat this inhuman game, she says. You must tame its dark forces and be victorious! Not just for me, Anu, but for all of us.

She laughs. Looks at Anu. Kisses the quarter and hands it back to him.

Oh you know, Jennifer says, have fun.

Jennifer turns and starts walking away. Anu watching.

See ya, wouldn't wanna be ya, Jennifer calls back at him over her shoulder.

Death looks at the quarter in his hand. On one side some Greek- or Roman-looking woman is holding a shield in one hand and a sprig of something in the other, her head turned to the right. IN GOD WE TRUST, it says, 1927. On the other side a Bald Eagle is in flight, E PLURIBUS UNUM.

Out of Many, One.

I am One, Death thinks, I am Many.

Death flips the quarter in the air. Catches it. Makes it move in between his fingers.

Death closes his eyes and when he does, he is everywhere at once. He is in California stepping into the path of the BART train, he is in North Korea several miles underground in the nose cone of a missile, he is in Ireland lying in bed at the Two Oaks senior care facility looking out the window at a crow who has just landed in the parking lot where a squirrel has been run over, he is in the crow, he is in the breast of a forty-five-year-old swimming coach getting a mammogram she has put off, he is in the hands of a brand new teen-age father who's tired and angry and shaking his baby. He opens his eyes again.

INSERT ONE QUARTER FOR ONE PLAYER / TWO QUARTERS FOR TWO PLAYERS.

Death lets the quarter slip into the slot. Ms. Pac-Man appears in the middle of the grid and soon after the ghosts are off and running, looking for blood. Death is finding his rhythm. He moves through the levels of cherries and strawberries, oranges. He loses a life when the pretzels appear but he's gained an extra life. He moves through apples and levels up to pears. He breaks through his own ceiling and the bananas appear. He moves through the bananas and then the oranges come back, strawberries, pears and then the pretzels come back. It's random. A tossup.

Death has been playing long enough now that a small group forms around Death. Other fifteen-year-olds like him, with clothes and oily skin and acne like him. They start rooting for him, encouraging Death to go further.

I'm on a quest, Death thinks.

I'm coming for you, universe.

His right hand is getting tired. Starting to cramp up. So is his left calf. Little seizures like small earthquakes move up and down both his legs.

The crowd around Death has grown. The whole of the arcade is watching him, spilling out into the upper level of the mall. Now other shoppers, adults with their shopping bags, with their children in tow, are stopping too, watching Death move this yellow ball with a mouth and bow in her hair around the grid. The crowd keeps growing. It moves in from as far away as the Macy's and the food court, the Hot Topic. The escalators have stopped. Everyone's mesmerized by Death, everyone cheering Death on.

How long has he been playing? An hour? Several hours? A day and a night? A week? A kid near him lifts a soda up so Death can drink from the straw. Another kid holds a slice of pizza just below Death's field of vision so he can eat. He feels like a god. He can see his score clicking by, getting higher and higher. 634,220 and then 798,567. Rising like a kite. 891,640—*click click click*—910,378—*click click*—930,847—*click*—933,580—*click click click* . . .

It feels like the crowd around Death has stopped breathing.

If only Jennifer could see this, Death thinks.

Death has one life left, one Ms. Yellow-Ball with a bow in her hair.

The crowd leans in, in unison. Eyes open. Mouths open. Death maneuvers Ms. Pac-Man out one of the side doors on the grid and she reappears suddenly on the opposite side, eats a cherry and then a ghost—*click click click*. His score turns in slow motion and 1,000,000 flashes on the screen.

The crowd erupts.

Pompeii, Death thinks, fucking Pompeii!

Fuck yeah, he yells out above the clapping and cheering, Fuck you, universe, I'm the fucking god of the universe!!

The crowd cheers.

Then something odd happens on the screen. The screen starts to click out and then his score clicks back to zero.

Click.

Death's mouth opens, what the fuck is that???

A loop, thinks Death. Wait, this is all just a loop? No no no no no no no no no. Death feels cold and sweaty, and the sweat is like ice water.

The universe, me, all these people, none of it matters. Is that what this is? Death wonders out loud. The universe makes you think it all matters but it doesn't?

A ghost passes through one of the side doors on the grid and eats Death's last life.

I'm dead, says Death, to himself but also to everyone else around him.

He's so tired he feels like crying. He looks at the crowd, which is looking at him.

We are all dead, Death says, quietly, almost unbelieving, None of this means anything. He looks at the kid closest to him. None of it, it's all just nothing. Then a little louder, You hear me? Death says, It's all meaningless. You, me, all of us.

PARENTAL DREAM

In this dream Carl has his parents back,
back in a green kitchen

in Illinois. And Mark, Mark
has his father back

and is walking with him
right now in London,
holding hands beneath the gray

and white, needlepoint sky.
In this dream I am dying

and my children are filling
up an IV bag with red
Jell-O which, in the dream

I am having, is medicine.
In this dream Mike's mother
remains alive

and the cancer she has fought
off for years

gets washed away in a small
load of laundry
filled mainly with her husband's
socks and underwear.

In this dream Dorianne's
mother and Joe's older brother
who was very like
a father both drive up in the same car.

My youngest bends over
the bed and pats me on the cheek
and says

*poppa this medicine is going
to work 'cause it's really yummy.*

My oldest sits at the foot
of the bed and says

*this is not going well, I think
we should just stop.*

In this dream Sharon's father
comes back but changed, kinder,
a man who only loves,

and my mother's father
comes back too, still horribly

young and sits with his now
older-than-him daughter
and asks where his wife is

who just then walks into
the room in a blue summer dress
holding a porcelain bowl
of fat blackberries

and hands them to my oldest
son and says

feed these to that man in bed,
he has no idea
about the living or the dead.

A PASSING

—in memory of Ernie Casciato

You died in the morning and time
did not stop. You were breathing

and a nurse passed by your door
in wintergreen scrubs

and then you were not breathing.

Your death being like any death,
invincible with Hitchcockian shadows
passing over your hand
where the IV port no longer

had a job to do. Whatever pee
you had left in your bladder
passed through the urinary catheter
and into the man-made lake

of a plastic bag
which was lying
next to you on the bed. As still as a lake.

Yellow water.

Water that has been
fuzzed-up with electrolytes,
potassium, and phosphorus.

When my four-year-old
is at his mother's house
I will sometimes pick up
the cotton pajamas he wore
the night before
and bury my face in them

before passing through
the three rooms in my house
to drop them
into the laundry basket.

When your brother called me
to tell me you had died
I had just passed the table
where my kids were eating breakfast.

My oldest passed his fingers through his hair.

Outside your hospital window
in the afterlife of you
no longer being on earth

a garbage truck ran a stop sign
but passed through

traffic unscathed, a squirrel passed
between one branch to another and when it did
its tail caught a little bit

of the morning light
sparking through the leaves.
The family of another patient

passed a cigarette
back and forth on a bench.

In your room dust floated
in the light, swirled
over the machines,
passed over your feet,
your knees,

swam through the air
in their particular code, some landing
on your lips, your closed
eyelids, your forehead, but most of the dust

simply passed over your body
and landed, softly, somewhere else.

OCEAN BOUND

Kelsey Yoder

Moreschi & Sons Antique Accordion
$99.00

This is a 1930s accordion by the Italian company Moreschi & Sons. It is in working condition though one key sticks if not pushed hard enough or, let me be honest, you haven't had enough to drink. The front is missing some diamond-like inlay, and the case is battered and taped. You can see all of this in the photos. My father played it happily for some years before my brother and I were born. He would play drinking songs for my mother when they'd just begun to date, to court, ending each song with his one line of Hungarian, knowing it made my mother blush and glow with honor that he'd learned a few words just for her—*Fogd be és csókolj meg!* he'd shout, *Shut up and kiss me.* And she would. My mother was rosy then, her green eyes as pure as a soybean field in May. And my father stood tall, despite the weight of his drinking. My father bought a farm, worked the land and built our house from brick. He stopped speaking Hungarian shortly after the marriage in 1952, and my mother (it took her much longer) stopped shutting up. My younger brother Richard and I never learned to play. This is a large, heavy, and fragile item—I will only ship it, in addition to the agreed cost, throughout the contiguous forty-eight after payment is received.

Vintage Daisy B·B Gun
$80.00

"Shoot this realistic western-style saddle carbine. You'll have more fun—you'll really be somebody—with your own Daisy in your hands!"

This mint condition classic Daisy B·B gun from 1965 is priced to sell quickly. See the painted chestnut finish and plastic stock; it's new and never shot. I opened the box for the first time, with great care, to check the pieces and parts—they're all here: manual, certificate of ownership, and one tube of BBs included. My brother Richard remembers receiving this gift for his seventh Christmas. By this time, Richard had left school. At the end of the first grade, the teacher, Mrs. Phillips, called a meeting, and she announced to my family that she would not pass my brother to the next grade. My father stood, taller than her, and told her she had to. *How can I pass someone whose voice I've never heard?* she asked. My father shouted at Richard to talk, sing the ABCs. Mrs. Phillips was lovely, jet-black hair set in waves, but her beauty never left an impression on Richard. My family left with the plan that my mother would begin homeschooling, but by Christmas, she'd already given up. Richard was allowed to meander the farm and read, all he has ever wanted to do. Now, Richard is labeled socially inept, an introvert, on the Autism spectrum. Then, he was called dumb, retarded, fatty-fatty-four-eyes. That first spring, Richard wandered down to the swimming hole alone and I was sent to find him. When I did, a pack of four boys, their necks craned, stood beneath the black maple, its branches reaching out over the Wabash River, one side of the bank Illinois, the other Indiana. There was a branch with a rope swing tied to it, a loop at the bottom for a foot. Richard was up the tree, way up, trapped like a coon, his eyes black and beady. The boys were swinging the rope up to Richard, telling him to catch it—*Put it around your neck*, they yelled, *Jump!* I screamed, and that was enough to convince most of the boys of their wrong. But one, Chris Baxter, tried to tell me they weren't doing what I thought they were doing. I punched him below the belt, felt my fist there like a suction cup. They ran. That night Chris Baxter's mother called, and I could hear her screaming through the telephone as my mother held the receiver away from her ear—*Your daughter has made my son infertile!* Not so, Chris Baxter has two children now by different women. So I was relieved when Richard was pulled from school—I had grown weary of protecting him, of being called to his classroom with a fresh pair of pants or a paper bag; he would be safe. I see now that my parents, presumably my father, were making a statement with this gun gifted to Richard a month after the Pentagon told President Johnson that American troops would have to be tripled to neutralize the Viet Cong forces. Had it been my gift, if I'd had it at the river that day, Chris Baxter would tell a different story, but not so Richard. In sixty-one years he has never even broken the spine of a book. He returns every item in the same condition he received it, and this B·B gun is no different. Everything you need is in the box. I'm happy to mail it, cost plus postage, and I'll remove this posting as soon as it's sold. Once it's yours, we're free of it. We won't be bothered by your decisions, whether to hang it like a stag above your mantel or gift it to your seven-year-old son to safeguard or bludgeon.

Children's School Desk with Matching Chair
$25.00

Child-size play desk made in Cook County in the 1950s with the original oak chair, sturdy metal legs, and wood top that rises to set at two different angles. The lower angle is good for hiding items quickly; the higher angle works well as an easel for art projects. In the pictures, you'll notice some imperfections, all easy fixes: a dash of red paint on the top, a dent in the right leg from being set too close to a door, and the wood of the backrest has begun to crack. This is the humid Midwest, and this item has not been locked away in a temperature-controlled storage shed. However, the cracking of the chair stems from my father's consistent rocking. He was a smart man and wanted me to be smart, too. He would sneak up behind me while I worked at the desk and rock me onto the back legs, my feet coming into the air and my pen rolling across the floor. In this way, the papers on the desk became visible from behind. If I were doing good work, he'd run his hand through my hair and peck me on the cheek. If I were not doing the correct work—journaling, writing poems—he would take the papers away to the fireplace, add them to the burn pile, and return to kiss me, pushing into my flesh as if he could leave a stamp. With time, I outgrew the desk, though I tried not to. When I could rest my breasts on the top and lean forward, completely obscuring my work, my mother told me I had to move to the kitchen table—*You're growing crooked*, she said. At sixteen, I sat in the dining room with my algebra homework, and my father leaned in. I pulled away. What was different this time? I had outgrown him, too. He grabbed me by the hair, slapped me across the face with his free hand, said, *I'm allowed to kiss my daughter*. And he did, pressing into the burning red mark of his hand, then releasing me. *My daughter*, he said and walked away. I told my mother; she nodded, listened, and when I finished she walked away too. I didn't seek the response I thought I deserved from my best friend, my boyfriend, or my brother. My love for school came early, through play, then the real thing, and then the need to be anywhere but home. Here, the story lends itself to the fact that I was a straight-A student, graduating third out of fifty-two. This desk has the potential to make your child more productive, and more visibly so. Contact me before purchasing to determine the proper shipping amount. I am willing and able to deliver this item—free of charge and swiftly—within 50 miles of Charleston, Illinois.

Leather and Brass Dog Collar with Plaque
$16.00

Here is a 1960s-era dog collar made from leather with a brass buckle, D-ring, and four rosettes. The leather is supple, but one section of brass has some dents, as shown in the close-up photo. The collar measures 1¼" wide and 24" stretched end to end. The brass plaque is engraved with the name Luke but could be replaced. All day my father worked in the fields and Luke, loyal Luke, his coat a coarse salt and pepper, my father's one true friend, slept beneath the big oak, never leaving the shade. My father would sit next to him at lunch, open a can of sardines, and Luke would wake. They'd split it; then Luke lapped at the empty can, the ragged edges cutting his tongue, so he drank more blood than juice. This is the same oak tree my best friend Karla and I tied Richard to while playing cowboys and Indians. Of course, Richard was the lone cowboy. We left him there, the trunk keeping his back straight, from lunch until dinner. Richard, the same silent child at age seven as age ten to the dismay of my parents, didn't cry, yell, or struggle. He waited, looking up into the leaves, accepting willfully that this was the life of a cowboy. I stood at the kitchen window with Karla at my side and watched my father cut the rope. Set free, Richard fell to his knees as if to pray, and I could tell my father was yelling by the waving of his hands. When I turned to Karla, she giggled nervously. *Go home*, I said. Luke received my dinner that night; it was venison pot roast with carrots and green beans, and I sat at the table while my family ate. Occasionally, I caught my father talking with Luke, rubbing his ears with a patience no other family member received. I can recall the day Luke died, the first time I saw my father cry. Luke was buried beneath that oak, but the land no longer belongs to our family. My father sold the farm at the age of sixty-four. He, my mother, and Richard moved to town for health reasons—doctors' appointments, hospital proximity, and a nursing home if it ever came to that. It didn't come to that: I was there, coming and going from their house every couple of days. I can only imagine how much my father paid for this collar initially—it's a steal. There is no farm now, no dog, no use for this collar. I'm happy to ship this small and relatively light item anywhere for a small fee.

Lot of Three Keepsake Stuffed Animals
$12.00

For sale, set of three stuffed animals from the 1970s: an orange lemur, a purple crocodile, and a red mouse with very oversized ears. Each animal has embroidered facial features and tags punched through a toe or a paw. The colors may seem odd now compared with today's more life-like versions. This only makes them more charming, mystical, and collectible. These items are not recommended for children, as they should not be machine-washed and certainly contain dust by now. My boyfriend in high school, Jesse, was raised as a Jehovah's Witness, and though he no longer attended service at Kingdom Hall, during the two years we dated—Junior to the day after graduation—he never gave me a present for my birthday or Valentine's. Instead, he gave me a stuffed animal approximately a month later. These gifts were never wrapped. When I opened the door of his Studebaker after school, the creature sat crooked in the passenger's seat, tossed like a cigarette butt out a window, and he'd say, *You can have that.* I set them on a shelf in my room, never to be played with, slept with, cuddled. I was far too old, but a few times, I caught Richard rearranging them, cooing ever so softly, shaking and brushing the dust from the brightly colored coats. It's clear to me now that I never knew Jesse. Yet, he did come to know Karla, my old best friend, quite well. Karla often caught a ride home with Jesse and me; she'd smoke cigarettes in the backseat while he smoked a joint, and I chatted on about books and people. They went away to Joliet Junior College, like many students before and after, not quite ready for an entrance into the Windy City. I chose not to attend college; there was too much to do at home. Instead, I began work at the public library, which my mother approved of. Richard did, too, and I picked his books for him: *The Hardy Boys*, *The Boxcar Children*, *Nancy Drew*. Karla and Jesse were married the summer after their college graduation, and though I was invited, I did not attend, not out of animosity, merely lack of time—Richard needed me, his neck swollen that day from having his tonsils removed. I expected to hear of Jesse and Karla's new life, their children, any day. Two years later and no kids, word trickled downstate that Karla was having an affair with a man from her office at State Farm Insurance. Divorce proceedings began, made clear by Jesse's return to his parents' home quite regularly on weekends. I never spoke to him, had no interest. All news made its way to me at my post, piled high with returned books. The news came: Jesse, heartbroken, about to be alone, hanged himself from the exposed rafters of their small Craftsman home, and Karla found him there. I wrote her a letter I never sent, filled mostly with quotes, hardly a word of my own. I can remember one line: "Where is the sea that once solved the whole loneliness / Of the Midwest?" At that time, I was having a fierce affair with James Wright's work. I wasn't talking about me; I was talking about her, but I realized this wasn't clear and burned the letter. It's been years now since these furry animals were around cigarettes and marijuana, but there's something about them that will always seem drug-addled. Still, they are in impeccable condition, and more so, I'm downsizing. Even Richard has out-grown them. They need a new home, your home. Easily packaged, easily shipped; I'll even cover postage.

Church Hymnal Titled "Christian Life Songs"
$7.00

The inside reads: *"For Sunday School, Praise and Prayer Meetings, Congregational Singing, Christian Endeavors, Special Meetings, Choir & Home."* When was the last time your family sang hymns around a fire?

This volume of church hymns, "Christian Life Songs" published in 1971, is in decent condition despite time and carelessness. The cover shows slight surface wear and corner creases and features a rough wooden cross on a star-strewn background, evident in the close-up second image. The hymnal is intact though there is visible wear, discoloration, and tanning to all of the pages but thanks to the little use it's been for numerous decades, all 233 pages are accounted for, plus an index. I imagine the book was borrowed from the church by my mother, who worshiped there every Sunday, although it's possible my father could have taken it much later as well. My mother believed my unwillingness to grant them grandchildren saved my father's soul from hell. He called me frigid; he called me a prude; he nicknamed me Prunie at the age of twenty because he loved children. My mother told him over Sunday brunch one afternoon that Mrs. McDowell, the local seamstress and babysitter, retired from her duties in the church nursery. He immediately offered his service. Of course, there was an unspoken rule at the First United Methodist Church, and my father, having listened to my mother prattle on about so many things concerning the congregation knew his working alone with the children would be frowned upon. It didn't help that he only attended church on Christmas and Easter. So, my father told my mother she must join him. She huffed at the demand: *I'll make a deal, old man,* she said, *One Sunday in the nursery for one day of you sitting through the full sermon.* He was appalled, pleaded.

That's the deal, she said. He should have appealed to my mother's work ethic, how she'd be appreciated by all, but he was selfish. His last Easter, we sat in maroon-covered pews, shoulder to slumped shoulder, and he whispered in my ear: *You sure sweat like a whore in church but you've got nothing else to show for it.* Granted, it was unusually hot that spring, but this item must go before I use it for kindling. The attached images are of the exact book you will receive. Contact me anytime, make an offer day or night, and make it soon. Free shipping. It can be yours.

Large Oceanscape Oil Painting
$5.00

Originally purchased from a rummage sale at the local Catholic Church, this detailed oil painting of a lighthouse, the ocean, and the rocky coast is for sale, again. The painting features pastel colors and the soft, visible lines of Impressionism. The sun is setting, the colors bleeding into the water, and one could assume this is the west coast, the Pacific Ocean. Purchase includes the frame, glass, and ready-to-hang wire on the back. The initials "J.M." are in the bottom left corner of the painting, visible in the attached pictures. The painting hung in my parents' modular home over two consistently reclined chairs. It is the ocean my father and mother will never see. Late in their lives, my parents dreamt of travel—Florida especially, always the achievable goal of the Midwesterner. I, too, daydream of the ocean from behind my desk, but not this ocean, not their ocean. In the winter of my twenty-second year, I went home to prepare our house for a blizzard. We carried firewood on sleds and left every faucet in the house dripping, a fan pointed at the exposed pipes beneath the kitchen sink. That night, snow drifted up fifteen feet around the house. The next morning, Richard and I donned our winter mittens and hats. We opened the window of his bedroom, and tunneled into that drift, using two of Mother's plastic bowls for shovels. We made rooms, a whole home. Richard took the blanket from his bed, pulled it through the window frame into our space, and I curled around him, we were safe and warm. We listened to the wind as it made waves, and drifted higher. We looked at the snow, looked into it, past it, and knew it was made up of waves. It was our ocean. Our father began to shovel a path, somewhere outside us, making little progress. We heard the scrape and the heaving of the snow over his shoulder. We laughed like children, and we were at that moment, ten and thirteen again; it was as if I'd never tied Richard to that tree, never left him there alone. And inside our big, white room, the snow melting at our touch, we shouted—*You can't shovel the ocean! You can't shovel the ocean! You can't!* I'm sure my father couldn't hear us; we were underwater, our speech making bubbles that popped at the surface. Richard and I have seen the ocean, the way the sun turns it pink and orange; we've felt how cold it is at the bottom, how warm it can be floating together. We have our ocean—we don't need theirs, we don't need this painting. We need so little. The painting is large, 22x30, too large I think to be worth shipping, the hassle of safe packaging, and waiting in line. If you want it, come and get it.

Off-White Ceramic Coffee Mug
$2.00

Used 10 oz. ceramic coffee mug, the inside scoured clean. One side has the name of the business, "Ford Thompson's Drug Store on the Square," followed by the address and phone number printed in red. The other side is left blank, off-white, yellowish-white. There are no chips, no cracks, just a reminder of other old things. I was finally prepared to return this item, but Ford Thompson's Drug Store closed three years ago. I met my father there for lunch two weeks after my fortieth birthday. We sat at the soda fountain counter, watching Lori, the constant lone lunch woman, scoop the special of beef and noodles over mashed potatoes. We sat with our backs to cold cream, cough suppressants, and ankle braces. The seats were full, up and down, the farmers talking of rain and yield. I stared into my coffee and my father stared into his Cherry Coke. *Where's Richard?* I asked. *Are you dating?* said my father. I shook my head. *Why not?* He looked at me, waited. *I'm content*, I said as Lori sat two heaping plates in front of us, then adjusted her hair net. *Anything else?* she asked, her smile dropped. *No, thank you*, I said and turned to my father—*What is it you want?* I knew the answer. *More*, he said. I hear him say it now, *More*. Do it for the family: my father, my mother, my Richard. Someone needs to come next, to carry on. My father's hair had turned white long ago, his muscles had become slack. I asked the question to move on to other topics and left without eating, the beef and noodles were left to gray and harden. But I took the mug. When it didn't fit in my car's holder, I dumped the coffee from my open window and let the cup roll around my backseat for a year. It dried with time, as I, having never wanted children, dried from the inside out. He sold the farm seven months after our lunch. The house was torn down, the trees uprooted, the soil tilled, the land merged with the neighbors' plot. Ford Thompson's, last of its kind, is a relic of the past and will never be resurrected. This is your chance to own a piece of history at a fair price. What's fairer? Free shipping on this and any additional item you purchase from my listings—create a bundle, consider taking it all.

Slippers Spray-Painted Bright Green
$1.00

One pair of unisex beige, faux sheepskin slippers spray-painted the brightest green, for sale. The adjustable strap, though painted over, can still be modified on these one-size-fits-most shoes. The purchase does not include a box or tags, as there are none. I used to search endlessly for the perfect gift to give my father. These slippers were such a gift, the ultimate selling point being it was Christmas morning, and I had run out of time. The slogan shouted from the rack: "Comfortable as an Old Friend—From Day One!" My father, in the last years of his life, found it too difficult to tie his shoes and began, also, to feed the baby doll from my mother's closet. It was a doll I played with when I was young, and at first, I found it to be another awful tactic to induce procreation. But my father began demanding that Matilda, the doll, share dinner with him, my mother, and Richard. He would fall asleep on the couch with Matilda in his arms. He would cry out when he thought my mother was mistreating Matilda: *Why haven't you fed her?* And one day, my mother realized the doll was more important than she. My mother locked the plastic baby in the trunk of their sky blue Buick, which my father no longer had access to. He became restless, angry, and fled the house. My mother called me at the library: *I took his baby, now he's gone, he's left me.* She was crying, and I reassured her I'd find him, he hadn't left her, he'd only forgotten her. She didn't hear me, couldn't hear me: *He ran outside without a coat.* It was twenty-one degrees outside with a windchill of ten blowing across the open prairie. I left my post at the front desk to search for my father. I drove up and down snowy streets calling his name while winding toward their small suburban house of two bedrooms, my parents' and Richard's. I knew my father: he would be making his way out of town to the woods or the fields. I stopped at the house briefly to soothe my mother. Richard was there—he, too, unable to be left alone. My mother sent me out for boots to tromp the fields. I swung open the side door to the garage, and my father's voice croaked: *You—you can help me.* He held out these slippers. His feet, I noticed as I took the shoes in my hands, were bare and blue and so small on the cement of the garage floor. He took a can of neon green spray paint, a can he used in the past to mark items for removal on the farm, shook it with all his strength, and began to soak the shoes and my hands. I coughed, felt sick, felt sticky, but I didn't let go. When he finished, he ran his fingers through his hair as he used to after a long day of work. A thin strand stood at attention with a fleck of green on the end. My father cried, one tear rolling down the creases of his cheek. I set the shoes on the floor to dry, then steered my father by the elbow into the house. He went to bed asking for Matilda, and I promised she'd be back by morning. Perhaps the bright green paint on the slippers will fade with wear, and become distressed, the tan showing through. Take them if you want them. There is no need to be gentle.

Collection of Baby Socks
$ FREE

Thirty-seven pairs of tiny socks—one pair for each year beginning in 1972 and ending in 2009—never worn, never needed. Socks for every occasion: dancing flamingos, fresh spring strawberries, baseballs and bats, stripes and polka dots, sewn-on bells, grippers on the bottom so the feet don't slide across a smooth floor, but there are no itty-bitty feet. Will these socks ever be used, ever be worn to threadbare and holes for tiny toes to poke through? It's up to you. Although it didn't work for me, giving a pair of baby socks to your child each Christmas could spur them toward procreation. You can be confident they'll understand the meaning behind the gift, year after year. Or perhaps you already have a baby and they could use more socks. Why not? They're free. It was rare that my father went shopping, but two days before Christmas he'd make his way down to JCPenney's for a pair of socks. Though he made clear he'd prefer me to have a son, he did not seem to care much: the socks range in color, style, and size. I think my mother must have felt it necessary to carry on the tradition after my father was no longer mentally capable of such malice. But with him gone, her gone, the unusable sock-giving has ceased. A few days after Richard was born, I held him in my arms. I twirled his soft toes between my thumb and index finger, and he looked up at me, blankly. He was beautiful—black hair, black eyes. I loved him then, and I love him now. But I knew we were different. If he could, he would have made my father happy, and I wouldn't give my father the one thing he wanted. Richard is here, somewhere in the library as I type, post, and scan the inside flap of hardcover novels. He wanders up and down the three floors, picks a book, reads the first page, and slides it back to its assigned spot. Or perhaps he's grown tired of that now after seven hours. Perhaps he's sitting, flipping through the pages of a travel guide, *The American Tourist* or *Coastal Cities*, places we don't need to go, don't need to see. He is silent and feels safe here in the library, as most days there are only a few other people on the same floor as him, and he reminds himself often that I've come home from this job every day for over forty years. And I'm here—I'm here, Richard; I'm not leaving. He wanders and reads, making his way through a sea of books, and I sit behind this desk. These tiny socks are free. Everything is free. Let us be free, free of all this. Please take them. Only, leave us this: On the drive to our warm home, Richard will share what he has learned from the books, what he has seen, and I'll be able to see it, too—the coral reef, the silverfish, the sailboats, the sun reflecting off the great body of water. Only leave us our ocean.

Michael McGriff

Excerpts from a book-length poem,

INQUEST

Was that the sound of my brother
getting arrested? Or was it

the moon collecting its debts
from the jimson weed? Perhaps

it was the surf throwing itself
into the jetty, failing to strike

a blue spark? Lovely ghost, is that you
at the end of the driveway trying

to convince the young deputy
that a set of brass knuckles

is only a paperweight, or have I fallen
asleep with the windows open,

overhearing the thorn apples
swap stories as the ocean shuffles

its eternal deck of black cards
in the last corner of summer?

*

Was that my grandmother
restringing her fiddle,

or were those alder branches
scraping the downspout?

Do the moths hold grudges
against the wings of the moon?

*

If it's true that ghosts don't shit,
is it also true their jokes are terrible?

Was it real, when I heard
the trees comparing their debts?

Does the river wear gloves
when it dismantles a foot?

*

Why do I value the physics of a spark plug
more than the mouth of a scholar?

Is the fog on Blue Harbor jealous of gas and oil
mixed and burned into a trail of blue smoke?

Was that a wild turkey accosting an old woman,
or was that a man dancing with an ironing board?

*

Shoveling this manure, why do I feel
suddenly related to half the phone book?

How is the fresh paint on the black hinge
related to the crows stripping the tree

of its cherries? What is a parabola
if not the arrogance of symmetry,

and why do the cut halves of a sour apple
spin in opposite directions on the butcher's block?

*

Have you already discovered the walls
are stuffed with straw and newspaper,

or are you still dancing to the radio
unplugged since 1941? Why is it today

that all women see their dead sons in me
the moment I slouch through a doorway?

Where did the hidden star keep its sack
of stripped bolts as it crept through the night?

*

Why don't these canyons' painted hills
yell at me to hear their own voices?

Did the sheep in Sweden get so lost
they became the clouds my grandfather

tried to remember? If I keep scouring you
with kerosene, will I reveal the face of a deer?

*

How long is the equation between
the moon and this handful of rice?

Did I mention there are dead beetles
in my new pack of smokes, that the bones

in my hand have grown thin and blue
as the first snows in the Year of the Rabbit?

*

Was that an owl or *Bicycle Thieves*
projected onto the side of our barn?

Was that the back door or an old record
hissing beyond its final track?

Or was that the crunching of gravel
just past the end of the pavement?

*

Does the common rat
support organized labor?

Is the smoke hidden inside a box knot
different than the smoke in a square knot?

Do you remember how we drove to town
to watch our father buy Red Wing boots

with his first paycheck from the mill?
How many rivers will refuse to vote

in the primaries? Did the runoff
from the upstream chrome plant

turn the ferns orange as an eyelid
in the October moonlight?

*

Is the river deep enough to swim?—even
if it tucks a dark feather behind its ear?

Is it trespassing if you find a cloud
with its iron mouth pressed to the water?

How often is a dead man's eye fitted
to the milky head of a floating shad?

Is the hatch a winged shape shaped
by how we swim along the shore?

*

Will it be trees or factories whose roots
grow down into my grave? What's it called

when a rope stretches two inches beyond
its limit? Will my final thoughts

reflect my pride over never using umbrellas,
or will I see a new mountain rise up from the sea?

Would I tire of crows if they finally wrote down
their opaque theories of the evening sky?

*

Maxine Scates

FALLING

The goats had fallen from a cliff, mountain goats,
two of them, tangled in kelp along the surf line.

This was long ago. They were surefooted, yet
somehow lost their footing, as if first one had fallen

and then the other, surprised by its companion's
sudden disappearance, took one step forward

and fell too, the way for weeks first the routine
of every day and then whatever we were looking

forward to has slid away. But our days
were already quiet. We did not lose our jobs

because we did not have them anymore. We had
no children and did not have to think of what

to tell them about what had already happened
or was happening or what might. Still, the feeling

in my gut is not unlike what I felt at thirteen
on the day of the week we ate meat when

the evening news was interrupted by the President,
a year away from his death, telling us we were

at the edge of a nuclear war. I could not eat.
I got up from the table and went to my room

as my mother called out, *Come and eat your meat.*
I did not, and it's what we did not know was coming

that still churns now because, like the goats and how
they fell, having never known how much time

we have left it seems we're somehow closer now
to knowing. Just a month ago we drove home

from the coast, the weathered pilings stood exposed
in the shallows of the Siuslaw River, and further on

horses bowed their long necks as they grazed. It was
a Saturday morning, in Mapleton cars gathered at a cafe,

and inside the diners sat at their tables eating
breakfast on an ordinary day.

WAYS OF SEEING

My neighbor, wearing his mask, was taunted
by two younger men in the grocery store who said,

It's only a virus old man, which surprised him,
as it does me, and since I'm of an age that means

I should be careful for now and my short forever,
I wondered what it was those men didn't want

to understand. My mask is blue with swirls on it
and reversible. Online, I saw a mask with penises—

the woman who wore it said if you were close enough
to see the penises, you were too close. Whereas,

if you are trying to ignore the virus, maybe you think it,
like your own fear, will go away with summer,

or ultra-violet light, or injections of bleach or any
other household disinfectant we've been inhaling for years—

poisons, like fear itself, being so much more familiar,
consoling, than the possibilities of science even as

the rest of us still hope for only a few years more before,
as the signs posted randomly around the neighborhood say,

This too will pass, and life as we knew it will resume.
And then, will we remember what we have learned

about being ready when it comes again? Or will life
as we knew it mean that the owners of meat packing plants

will still insist workers work so close to each other
that they knock elbows while the drug companies make

their millions from the vaccine because it's America
and that's how it is? The other day, I found a thirty-year-

old letter from my mother-in-law addressed to us in Italy
and used Google Earth to find the street in

Florence where we had lived. For a moment, I walked
down Via San Niccolo, and then I remembered

somewhere in the hills behind me was Galileo's house.
He lived there in his later years under house arrest,

sentenced by the Inquisition because he believed
the earth was not the center of the universe. And so,

I stood again reading the brass plaque on one of the walls
surrounding the house thinking of how, in his

confinement, Galileo might have stood looking through
the telescope he had invented, its powers allowing him

to see the craters of the unsmiling moon, the moons
of Jupiter, and the starred infinite fields of the Milky Way.

APRIL

The leaves I've dumped in the same pile for years
have turned into rich soil. I shovel buckets of it

around the eight-foot sapling sprung from the roots
of the oak cut down after last winter's late snow. I

hadn't noticed it until the old oak was gone. There
is so much time. I work more than usual among

the roses and rhododendrons I planted years ago. I
recall writing to a friend in a far away city on an

April day like this, the windows open for the first time
in months, Bill upstairs playing the piano, the cruelty

elsewhere then as now. A moment ago I saw my
grandmother again as she knelt to pray by the side

of her brass bed, the crucifix hung above it. I am five
or six and watch her from the cot under the eaves

where she has already tucked me in, and I feel like
I'm seeing something I should not see. Now, I know

it's that I will never know her. Today, it's Easter
Sunday and some insist they'll have their gatherings

despite warnings not to. This morning on the radio,
people reported on what they're doing, while like us,

they wait. One woman was walking her cat around
her backyard, a man was dying his hair, some were

lonely, some were trying to file for unemployment
and others worried their health insurance would run

out soon. The sick don't speak to us from their hospital
beds or nursing homes or shelters, their detention

camps along the border, their prisons or their small
apartments where paramedics say sometimes whole

families lie ill. If, at first, we thought the pandemic
the great leveler, the divisions among us live on as

I ready myself to walk out into another brilliant day
to sweep the pollen from the bricks while on Hart Island

three thousand miles away, the inmates from Rikers
dig trenches to bury the unnamed dead.

ONGOING

I've never known if it's enough
to remember the pattern of the maroon carpet
in the entry way at the top of the stairs,
how the light from the just opened door
fell on the roses, cabbage roses, I think, the kind
that bloom on sunny streets
a mile or so inland
along the central coast of California, whose
stems bend with the heaviness of their weight,
whose petals fall one by one.

~

A wild iris laid down in the snow.

~

Yellow headed blackbirds fell by thousands
from the sky because someone was there
to take a cellphone video of them falling.

~

We hiked in the mountains every summer.
Sometimes fields of paintbrush we did not lie
down in, sweat running down our backs,
our dog running ahead to the lake.

I slept in the hull of a boat at anchor, water
slapping the waterline all night. We sat on
an outcropping overlooking the desert
below and suddenly two jets blew by low
just over our head, or so it seemed.

Sometimes we got lost.

~

The stepping off place, the hesitation. We will
never say it as it happened. Whatever we make
will be as imperfect as we are, as worn, as broken,
as sewn back up.

~

Wikipedia says numbers are open to interpretation
but between ten and twenty thousand
civilians have been killed by U.S. drone strikes
since 2003 in Afghanistan, Somalia, Pakistan and Yemen.

~

It's hard to say what a view is like. I'd say
this coastline has not changed much
in all the years we have come here. The fishing boats
line the horizon at night as always, but this past
September the creek to the south was not
running down to the sea from the Coast Range.
On a day in April it is flowing. My dog
is starting to run more slowly. This morning
she was chasing the shadows of gulls flying
as lazily as kites. The creek to the north
is too wide to cross though there were years
we did cross when we walked all the way to the bay.
This morning a marten or fisher was making
its way up from the shore on the other side
of the creek. I was early and so was the animal.

No, it was going back to its den for the day
to avoid us. Once there was a coyote who asked
my dog to join it. Once there was a wolf held
by a string. We knew it was a wolf when the man
said, "He's not usually so good with dogs." The towhee
disappears into the seagrass beyond the bird box
I have not seen a bird enter. At dusk, the dove sings
the same song over and over on the other side
of the thin wall. Blue gives way to blue, no whales
here or in Crete where we rode motorbikes
polluting the air and the ears until we stopped
to eat oranges and chocolate under the olive trees
high in the hills. Crete, hills as tawny as a lion
as the ferry pulled into the harbor at dawn and
the smell of thyme rolled out to greet us. Hours later
a bus left us in the midday heat and we began
walking, lugging our bags uphill.

~

Everyone has memories.

~

They're bringing in a new general, the one
they call the Butcher of Syria.

~

We went down to the river because we had not
seen it all winter. The river was rushing and high.
The signs said No Camping. We went down to
the river because it was almost spring, still cold

at night, these raw days. Many others were
there, walking with their dogs, their children.
The babies were bundled, their parents wore
knit caps as they did elsewhere, crossing bridges
over rivers, crossing borders. The nuclear plant
was on fire backlit by flares. The mother, daughter,
son and a man who tried to help them cross dead
in the street, their small dog barking in its crate,
their wheeled bags upright. The invaders
bombed a maternity hospital. They called
the pregnant woman being carried on a stretcher
past the charred trees *a crisis actor*. A man found his
two cats in what was left of his house, his wife,
his daughter, his son-in-law, his twelve-year-old
daughter in her wheelchair, all dead. In the ruins
of the theater struck by missiles where hundreds
were sheltered one hundred and thirty survived.

NON-WORDS

Meli Hull

I sold copies of Margaret Wise Brown's *Goodnight Moon* to every customer who came into Tsunami shopping for baby shower gifts for five years straight without ever once cracking it open. At every baby shower I attended, parents-to-be were showered with multiple copies of *Goodnight Moon*. I always made a point to gift any other book but that one. I thought, this must be the only children's book these people have ever heard of.

Now, I rock my newborn daughter to sleep. I'm reading her the copy of *Goodnight Moon* we received at our own baby shower. It turns out that *Goodnight Moon* is . . . good.

I spend a lot of time now in the corner spot on my couch, breastfeeding my daughter. While this is happening, I've been half-watching the Netflix documentary series *Babies*. (Watching *Babies* while watching my baby. Learning about how babies learn while learning my baby.) One study featured on this show was designed to determine how babies figure out where words begin and end. Psychologist Jenny Saffran asked whether babies might be processing speech by tracking the "statistics of sound" to figure out which sounds go together predictably. To study this, she invented a language.

"It's a very simple language," she explains in the episode "First Words." "It just has a few made-up words in it. ... And there's no meaning in this language, because we wanted to start simple." The researchers would play audio of a monotone, synthesized voice repeating made-up polysyllabic "words" like *pabeecoo* and *golatoo* for the baby in a random order for two minutes. No meaning, but over the course of the two minutes, the baby would hear each word around forty-five times. After the two minutes were up, the testing room would go quiet, and a light to one side of the baby would start to blink. Once the baby turned to look at the light, audio would play repeating either a word from the made-up language, or a sequence of syllables that wasn't a word in the made-up language. (None of the "words" in either recording were words. Unintelligible. No meaning to speak of. Non-words.) The recording would continue to play until the baby turned its head away from the light. The babies who heard the "non-words" in the second part of the study looked longer at the lights than the babies who heard the "words." The prolonged looking indicates the babies' surprise to find the syllables in an unexpected order.

Babies pour the uninterrupted gush of speech into tidy cups of words through repetition. That's why you're supposed to talk to your newborn even though they can't understand what you're saying. Or *that* you're saying. That's why you're supposed to narrate everything you're doing as you carry them through the house, through their day. That's why you're supposed to read to your baby every day from the day they're born. To expose them to more words, more word boundaries, more statistics of sound.

But reading to a newborn feels like speaking the made-up language from the study. The words have meanings to me, but because she doesn't understand them, they die deaths of semantic saturation, become non-words. *Goodnight Moon* is nonsense, too, a nonsense poem I accidentally memorized after the fifth time through. Syllables in the same order every time that turn into words without meaning. I repeat them to her in the same order, with the same slow rhythm, bouncing her while she cries. Her face red and wet, eyes squinched shut, not perceiving the kittens or the mittens, the comb, the brush, or the bowl full of mush. I have become the quiet old lady who is whispering *hush*.

The pieces of our days, like the syllables that make the words, start to fall in the same order. Change her diaper, feed her, talk to her in her baby swing about pouring tea and toasting an everything bagel. "It's a bit of misnomer to call it an everything bagel. There are plenty of things that aren't included on this everything bagel. This is raisin bran, baby! One day you'll be able to eat raisin bran! I hope you like it! In the meantime, I'm going to turn this raisin bran into milk for you to eat." As soon as my breakfast is ready, like clockwork, she poops. (The baby swing puts her legs in the perfect position for pooping.) I put my tea and my bagel and my cereal on hold on the part of the counter the cats haven't figured out how to get to yet. I carry my daughter off to the changing table to change her diaper again. Afterwards, I set her in her baby bed on the kitchen floor. If I'm lucky, she falls peacefully into sleep while she watches me eat. If I'm unlucky, she screams at me. I explain that while she might not like it, I do have to eat food myself in order to create more food for her. I will feed her again as soon as I finish feeding myself. None of this means anything to her. I am exposing her to a high lexical diversity. This is the story I tell myself while I tell her the story of our days. Repeating, repeating.

Then she smiles at me on purpose for the first time. Then she develops a sense of humor. She learns how to blow raspberries, and how to giggle. New additions to our lexicon include calling diapers "dipes," and sticking my tongue out at her with a sound kind of like "nyeaahhh," and pursing my lips to blow raspberries at her so she'll mimic me, and asking her if she wants to "fly high in the sky" and then doing a cheerleading count-off of "one-two, down-UP!" as I lift her into the air. She squeals and giggles and opens her round mouth in a big grin. We repeat these non-words together. Through these repetitions, we make the meanings, together.

FARM LIFE

Ken Babbs

Hi.

My name is Bud.

When I was a high school junior, we rented a place we called Maple Island. Its old farmhouse sat under a huge maple tree in the middle of a walnut orchard by the river. The walnuts fed a wild little dog who lived under the house. She'd crack the shells open with her teeth. Scrawny and white with black spots, we named her Pepper Pot and almost tamed her with dog food, but she never let us touch her. An old barn in back had a Ford 8N tractor parked inside. Pepper Pot and that tractor lived there before we did, the farm's first inhabitants.

We kept a garden and chickens and me and my brother, Buddy, and my sister, Tilda, worked in the garden and took care of the chickens, too. We locked them in their coop at night—so the raccoons didn't get them—and collected their eggs and kept their chicken house clean. We let them run in the yard during the day.

That spring, Pop got the tractor started and began using it to pull a small trailer around the walnut orchard, picking up dead branches we used for firewood. Pepper Pot had puppies, and when they got big enough to come out from under the house we played with them. Unlike their mama, they became very tame. Soon as they were weaned we gave the puppies away, all but one, the littlest in the litter we called Tiny.

One day Pops was driving the tractor out in the orchard and he ran over Tiny with the big back wheel. He stopped and picked the puppy up. It was limp and unmoving. He breathed into its mouth, running for the house, the tractor still chugging where he left it. He put Tiny on a blanket next to the wood stove in the kitchen, then went back to the tractor. It had boiled over—lost all its water—and was making a clanking sound. He nursed it back to the barn and let it sit and cool off.

Tiny lived but the tractor died.

The landlord was not happy. Cost him six hundred dollars to get that tractor fixed. Pops didn't have the money to pay him back. He'd spent all he had buying Tilda an angry and stubborn Shetland pony. It didn't like to be ridden so Tilda quit messing with it. The pony, it wouldn't stay in the little pasture Pops fenced off, got out all the time, would go into people's yards the other side of the orchard. Pops would have to drag it home with a rope.

One time he got so mad at the pony he grabbed it around the neck. Back and forth they went, round and round, till finally Pops threw it to the ground and fell on top of it and wouldn't let it up, saying, *That'll teach you, you no good hay burning disreputable excuse for a godforsaken crittur.*

The pony hated Pops till the day he got a neighbor to take it away, free.

Our two roosters, Big Red and Big Black, never stopped fighting, Big Black winning every time, Big Red always scurrying. One time Pops was sitting on the back porch smoking his corncob pipe when Big Black pounced on Big Red from behind and started mauling him. Pops jumped up and grabbed Big Black, *I'll teach you some manners*, and holding the rooster tight, Pops puffed on his pipe and blew the tobacco smoke into Big Black's beak. He blew clouds into that bird for a while, then set Big Black down. The rooster staggered, dizzy and bewildered.

Pops nodded, *That'll settle things*, and walked back to the porch—which is when Big Red saw his chance, attacked Big Black and knocked him ass over teakettles, releasing the pent-up fury of having been beaten so many times. Pops turned to watch. He shook his head. *No way you can alter farm life, all you can hope to do is guide it to fruition.*

Pops got mad at the hog we raised from a weaner pig and wrestled it, too. He got up dirty and sweaty and puffing, *Gotta give up wrassling these critturs, they gonna give me a heart attack.* He butchered the hog, put an end to that fracas. That was the day the landlord served us an eviction notice. He was going to tear the farmhouse down, it was too old. Gave us thirty days to vacate. Pops said, *Shove your thirty days, we're staying until I find someplace else.* Damned if he was ever going to rent again.

We prowled the countryside in the old station wagon, Mom complaining, *How can we afford to buy a place?*

Just like every other broke Oregonian, Pop said, *Find us a stump farm and stick a single wide on it.*

He slammed on the brakes. *Bud,* he said, *Go see what that sign says stuck on that tree.*

I clambered out of the car and slid down the bank and slopped across a creek and up the other side, then back to the car again. *A for-sale sign,* I said.

Anything else?

A phone number.

Pop rummaged in the glove compartment for a scrap of paper and a pencil. *Go git that number.*

Pop sealed the deal over the phone. We packed up and moved out. *And you can forget that six hundred bucks,* Pop yelled at the landlord as we left Maple Island behind.

Our new five-acre place never got named, but it was covered with blackberries, some bushes halfway up big oak trees. Pop bought a couple of pigs, put an electric fence around two of the biggest blackberry bushes, and let the pigs loose inside.

My root-a-tillers, Pop said. *They're rooting for us.*

Mom planted a big garden on a bare spot the blackberries hadn't invaded yet. We added chickens and rabbits to the mix. Tilda was in charge of the hens; younger brother Buddy and I wrangled the rabbits. We had two does and a buck and they sure cranked out the babies, which we let grow up in an adjoining cage till they were big enough to knock on the heads. One slit down the belly and out with the guts, skin the hide off in one smooth move, nail it to a board, dry it out and sell it for six bits. The meat went in the freezer. Pop paid us fifty cents a rabbit.

Early in the mornings on bright summer days, Pop got us up and filled us with pancakes and announced, *Let's have a rock and roll party.* We groaned. He always followed that with, *You pick up the rocks or your heads will roll.*

While he worked on fencing off a big chunk of our five acres, Tilda and Buddy and I, carrying buckets, walked in a row across the field, picking up the rocks we found and putting them in the buckets. When they were full we carried them to the driveway and laid them down next to one another, creating two cobblestone paths wide enough for the car tires to travel on.

Pop bought a boar and, with two sows to service, we soon had lots of piglets. The sows were in pens next to one another. One day the boar was corkscrewing into a sow and the other one was watching. Didn't look happy about that state of affairs, being pregnant and all, seeing her old man rutting another femalian.

When the sow who witnessed the sordid event had her piggies, she wouldn't nurse them. Pop put the piglets to her teats but she just pulled away.

I was hiking home from across the road where we got our goat milk and Pop hollered at me, *Bring that milk over here, Bud.*

He sloshed it on the sow's teats and put a piglet's snout up to it.

The little feller started guzzling.

Pop splashed more goat milk on the teats and all the piggies began sucking.

Pop came home with a steer calf and a heifer. When the heifer came in heat he told me, *Bud, take the heifer up to the Andersons and get her bred.* I marched up the road, leading the heifer with a rope. I put her in a corral with the bull and climbed up on the top rail to watch.

Willa May, who was in my same grade in school, got up on the rail next to me. Made me real nervous. I was agitating and squirming watching the heifer and bull and finally couldn't contain myself.

Oh golly, I sputtered. *I wish I was doing that.*

Go ahead, Willa May said. *It's your heifer.*

Our house was on a flat spot on a hill. We had a big round table in the middle of an alcove that sat on stilts with the pasture below where the hogs and cows rooted and grazed. There was a big hole in the middle of the table with the ground open beneath. We shoved our uneaten food scraps down the hole for the pigs to eat. When they got so big they'd rear up with their snouts sticking up onto the table, Pop would say, *Time to butcher.*

Someone must have told the county about the pigs being under the house because an animal control officer came out and said we couldn't be doing that.

I'd like to know why not, Pop said, and the officer told him it just wasn't healthy.

That's a goldurned lie, Pop said. *We haven't lost a pig yet.*

The heifer became a cow and when her calf got big enough to wean, we put the litter feller in his own field. The cow was in the field with the pigs and one pig started nursing on the cow.

Pop shook his head. *Ain't nacheral*, he said, and stuck the pig in a pen—but it couldn't hold that critter, kept breaking through to get at the cow and her milk.

That ended it for the pig.

He became pork chops and ham and bacon.

It wasn't long until we got out of the hog business.

It had been raining for three weeks. Pop looked out the window and counted nineteen pigs wallowing in muddy pits, the pasture torn up like the middle of a world-war shelling. Pop called the stockyard and they came out with a trailer and loaded up all nineteen, the boar, the sows and all the young'uns.

They left the cow and a steer standing alone on the one dry patch in the pasture, a high spot on the far edge away from the creek.

The next year I went away to college and thought I left farm life behind—until forty years later when, as a grandfather, my daughter and her little son moved in with us, planted a big garden, got some chickens and bought a milk cow with a calf.

Now I'm building a pasture fence and a milk shed.

Looks like I'm back into farm life again.

NOTES FROM
MY FATHER'S BEDSIDE

Eve Müller

for Erik Muller

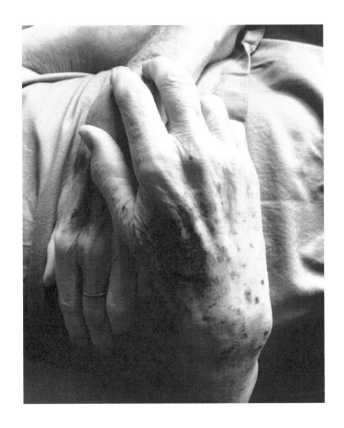

You lie propped in your hospital bed. I read from Roethke's note-books. *How far's my father now? Where has he gone, soft ears?* I ask you where *you'll* go. How I'll find you once you're gone. You speak of Lao Tzu's material cycling. Your hands twirl like pinwheels in the darkness.

*

You hold court from bed like King Henry VIII. Visitors stream past in coats and gloves. They bring with them blasts of cold, of life beyond this cloistered room. You open your eyes, pull yourself back from whatever strange place you're headed.

*

Leaves pile up on the deck outside the window. Whenever you turn your head you see heaps of maple, flashes of oak. You can't believe how much you're enjoying dying. "It's almost scandalous," you tell the hospice nurse, eyes brimming with red and gold.

*

Each evening, I give you a sponge bath. You are grateful for this simple ritual. You sit on your commode like a throne. Hot water runs down your back in rivulets. Your white body in moonlight, noble even in decay.

*

We meet in the night. I load my syringe with the electric blue liquid that will take you further away from us until all we can see of you is a bright speck on the horizon.

*

"You were an excellent father," I say. "Most of the time." We laugh until you start coughing. I hold a glass of water to your lips. We are past all that now. The countless small violences. The tiny hammer blows and surface wounds.

*

"I'm done with thinking," you say. And just like that you begin your disappearing act.

*

It's hard to get the words out. They stick in your throat like burrs. I lean in to hear you. In between this word and the next, this breath and the next, galaxies glide by. "I'm ready," you say. "I've *been* ready." We count the planets. We count their rings. You ask me why it goes on so long, death like some endless Russian film.

*

No one is speaking. The only sound the sighing of the oxygen machine.

*

Your granddaughter sits on the edge of your bed, offers you the cigar box full of harmonicas she finds in your drawer. Your lungs are shriveled, yet somehow you find the strength to play. Bent over the kalimba, she picks out the melody you are breathing into your Hohner Marine Band, shadows your every note. *Oh my darling. Oh my darling. You are lost and gone forever.*

*

You complain we are all clothed in black. To please you, I change into a velvet dress that shivers green and silver. Your eyes catch fire as you touch the shimmering stuff. "Who's the party for?" you ask. "For you, Dad," I say. "The party's for you." And I give you more water and a handful of pills.

*

"Bring me a beer!" you whisper-shout. I offer you a thimbleful of IPA. You take one sip, fall back against your pillow.

*

Words wash up on the shore of your brain. Less and less tied to the world where the rest of us live. It is fitting that you—a poet to the last—speak in koans.

*

Today you are sure we are making a movie. You speak of scripts, screens, bloody endings. "What if we end it with putting a knife through my heart?" you ask.

*

I am your angel of death. I fill your mouth with morphine, blue as autumn sky. But I forget. You no longer see color. The green of my velvet dress now lost on you. You shut your eyes and stroke my hair, speak of things the rest of us can't see. There are ghosts and trains and flashes of white light. You hear the mewing of a dozen cats. You see a pack of small black dogs filling up the room. You ask me how all my other patients are doing, smile wide as the fields when I tell you you're the only one.

*

Every few hours, the scratch of pen on paper. "Are you writing all this down?" you ask.

*

Your eyes are unfocused. Your brow damp with sweat. I can tell you're laboring to let go of us. To sever your ties to the clouds, to the hummingbird outside the window, to your daughter who can't stop pouring out tears. You never liked my tears.

*

You grab me by the wrist. Your milk-eyes lock with mine. "You're the one directing this film," you say. "*You* can make this stop." But I can't. You know I can't. I go into the kitchen so you won't see me cry.

*

Mom crouches on top of you. She is small as a cat. She whispers into your ear, kisses the lids of your eyes. You speak her name, "Ann," but your eyes remain closed.

*

I dim the lights, stretch out beside you on the hospital bed. We are both slender as reeds.

*

It is early morning. I wake just in time to hear your last breath. A soft chuffing. A flutter of wings. And then nothing left but open sky and the memory of birds.

*

Your body stiffens quickly. We cut off your clothes with scissors. I remove your watch. The dead have no need for watches.

*

I'm still reading Roethke, but your bed is empty now. The sheets blinding in their whiteness. I remember how you always spoke of Roethke. You gave me books, copied out poems by hand. They are gone now. Tossed aside. Sold at used bookstores to cover rent, buy bottles of gin and milk. Why didn't I read him? It would have made you happy, but I was young and wanted to have my own poets.

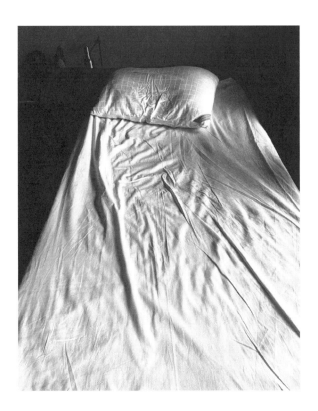

Erik Muller

A BOY'S EYES

{ a poem }

MORNING

Clete says "Shove over!" to his brother
and yanks shut the pickup door.
His father's hand trembles on the stick,
impatient to shift, get going—
August Sunday morning crew,
three about to enact the parable
of wood gathering, whose plot
is sinew and sweat, whose moral,
thrift. Oil and gas cans,
axe and maul rattle louder
once the truck hits gravel.
Town behind them now,
they climb green-filtered light.
The quick swap of sun
and shadow makes the Old Man
lean and squint, the coffee cup
clamped between his thighs
sloshing at every turn.
Maples curl their fingers.

Higher, firs of all ages
hold their breath, those near
the road powdered with dust.
Higher, the clearcut, crossed
pick-up-sticks of broken logs,
wood for the taking—
today a man and two sons,
a clatter of tools.
Before the saw leaps alive,
the father's voice telling
what sons need to do after
he bucks a log into rounds.
They nod, truck ticking,
heat beginning to stack tall,
bird whistle up where
a few firs are left standing.

HOW JAYBIRD SHAPED THIS LAND

Jaybird saw the people.
The people were coming.
They needed wood to build with,
to make their houses.

Jaybird sowed fir seed
across bare, flat land.
Overnight a forest
sprouted, tall in the sun.

Jaybird flew over it:
I will make more forest,
make forest enough
for people's houses.

Jaybird used his beak
to pluck up the forest
like a kerchief. With
his feet he wrinkled it.

Carefully he set it down
with folds and creases.
He made ridges and canyons
where rainwater could flow.

He made trees climb one side
and go down the other.
He made a bigger forest
with more wood for the people.

This morning Jaybird flies.
He looks down at clearcuts
and struggling seedlings.
He wonders, *Will there be enough?*

FLIGHT 73 TO NORTH BEND

You fly over the logged section
where Clete unloads tools
and waits at the tailgate
for orders. You can't see him,
the truck, a red spot.
You can't see the forest
in the forest that Burnt Mountain
cleared of significant wood,
leaving splintered fir, junk alder,
the ground brown as if toasted,
a dog blanket thrown to the floor
showing ripples and sharp folds.
Gullies of scoured stone.
You can't see foxglove, lupine,
huckleberry taking a chance
to thrive or shrivel.

The seatbelt sign blinks on.
The plane begins its descent.

IDLING

Just as the saw's idle
a throaty stutter
readies to blurt some crude thing
to rev and whine and whirl its teeth
against limb or trunk

so the Old Man's muttering Clete thinks
is ready to burst
lash out at anyone

WRENCH

No one else's father
has a name like it:
Wrench. Or a story of how
that name came to be.

The Old Man wasn't
the old man then,
simply all man.
Evenings at the tavern,
pool, cutting the deck
to see who'd buy a round,
now and then arm wrestling,
he started what became
a sport, a contest,
starting with a handshake.
Nothing unusual about that,
except two contestants
ratcheted from there.

Men stare and clasp hands.
They understand the aim:
build pressure, crumple
some fingers, squeeze
from bulging eyes a rear or two.

My father's unblinking stare
and poker face, his hand
a tightening wrench,
until through clenched teeth
his opponent must hiss,
Enough! I give.

That's how he got his name,
taking your hand in his,
gently at first, playful,
yet already too far
into the machinery.

SNARL & LEASH

To punish us he never
uses a belt. He looks pained
and politely asks for a hand.

It is not clear why he
strikes our mother. Something snarls,
something drives the Old Man.
Later she bows her head
over a bucket so she doesn't
bleed onto what she has to clean.
I'd rather have my own hand
crushed a thousand times
than see her hurt this way.

Next day at school
like a fool, I'm proud
to say, *My dad
is called Wrench.
What about yours?*

REAL NAMES

I'm Clete, named
for a Nebraska grand-
father I've never met.

Little Brother sounds
generic, but that's what
we call my little brother.
My mother is my friend
but I could never
call her Ada.

The Old Man, maybe
a stone-faced mountain
or the god on top,

I already explained
is known as Wrench.
Before that story

there was a boy
like me, spindly, blonde,
peering about

like me to find
a path steady
and good.

What do you think
his name was then?
Clarence! Clarence Reese Hanks.

This bull of the woods,
faller, cat skinner,
Buck Roller to crews,

got stove up bad,
knees, ankles, assorted scars,
then was assigned to the mill yard.

He boasts about glory days,
rolls up a pants leg
to exhibit his bit of history,

wounds red, white, and blue,
while every workday now
he climbs to the seat

of a company lumber carrier
(it goes by better names,
Jitney, Straddlebug, Bug).

There he perches, delivering
long boards and timbers,
A to B, B to C, touching

no thing sharper than an ignition key.
Up there for all the world to see,
he sure enjoys gunning it!

HUNTING POSSUM

After dark, possum wander
　　down from Breezy Hill
　　　　to the abandoned drive-in.

On tiptoe they come, nosing
　　near blind toward the market,
　　　　the dumpster aroma.

Clete stands
　　with two other boys holding
　　　　lengths of 2 x 4.

Three beams click on and rove,
　　catch blazing eyes,
　　　　silver hair of possum.

The boys move in,
　　one swings hard,
　　　　cracks a skull.

The possum stalls,
　　tips over,
　　　　completely still.

Beams search
　　for another one,
　　　　the first left in darkness.

Arms heavy and slack,
    the boys soon tire of it.
        "I'm gonna get a Coke.

Wanna come?"
    No answer. In a line they walk
        toward the market.

VIEW LOTS

A line of bright streetlights
tops the horizon of the hill,
the best view property
above the bay, the web of
the distant bridge. Shasta Way
named for the developer's child,
though paved, utilitied, well lit,
has yet no house with high
windows framing north light,
the metals of chill bay water.
Mills shut down when demand
for lumber slackens, a tide
on long, less predictable cycles
than the creep of brackish water
out and back across clay fats.
Shasta's father cut trees
for the mill on the slough
and bladed off topsoil
for a nursery to sell
to new homeowners
landscaping bare lots.

Breezy Hill view lots,
with city improvements,
sit ready, yet despoiled,
while three boys below
hunt possum in the dark,

boys whose Depression-
wandering grandfathers
brought possum from the South,
turned them loose near town
to be there for a hard time's hunger.

YOU BROKE IT

You broke it. Now fix it.

I didn't break it.

Somebody did. It wasn't broken before.

Not me. I don't even know how to fix it.

It needs fixing.

Who do you think can fix it?

I don't know. It's useless broken.

Maybe we should throw it out.

I didn't say that. Somebody could fix it.

Great. How do we find out who?

SHASTA SINGS

Though I know Shasta sings
the first time I hear her
is at the memorial for Randy,
who slid his car into the slough.

The whole school is there,
Randy's parents on stage
with the principal. Shasta
looks tiny and timid.

Randy was her friend.
Her voice, pitched above
guitar and drums, seems tiny, too,
searching for a landing place.

God's candle lights the darkness.
The Voice to whom my soul hearkens.

VOICE

Tides moving beside
the slough road
and in and out of culverts.
Suck of sewerage,
a hazy brew, then easy
exhale, sending bark chips
and chain scrabbling along
a slick clay bottom.
Culverts strained
by the weight of traffic.

SHASTA

The first time I talked
to Shasta was at a party
at her house on Breezy Hill,
a June evening when the sun
traveled so far north
it seemed it would never come back.

The party noisy on the deck,
we were in the kitchen together,
getting a pitcher of tea
and towels to wipe up a spill.
It was strangely quiet.

Like me, Shasta's short.
We were trying not to touch
when we passed between counters.
I don't know how we collided.
My hands shot above my head
as if to shout, "I didn't do it!"
We both muttered "Sorry."

She smiled and turned.
I watched her walk away,
the clearest view I'd had
of a girl wearing shorts,
her legs smooth and tan,
her flip flops with each step
a slow applause I was
feeling then for Shasta.

FLARE

Little Brother and I

do what the Old Man says,
moving the rounds he bucks
up or downhill to the truck.

The morning goes forward
slowly, like any morning
at school, while time

slips by much faster
when I set and reset
the shifter on my bike.

How long are storms in winter?

Or flowers I give Shasta
when I want to tell her
something I think is true.

A day with the Old Man
can creep along, then flare.

So, approaching noon,
my brother and I are bored
shouldering rounds.

Our hands, tired or simply
needing change, let one loose
on a run downslope.

It leaps and stumbles
like a shot coyote, now
tumbles like a stone

aimed straight at the truck.
The way on the lot where we play ball
a grounder hits a pebble and swerves,

so this round strikes something,
hops in air, deflects a bit
and clears the truck by a yard!

We hear it crash a path
through brush on the other side
of the road. Then still, like held breath.

The one wild one. The rest
we manage carefully,
grappling, applying brakes,

and lift them into the bed,
stacking and packing tight.
Until from uphill, a yelp—

Old Man himself jumping now
so bent and wobbly he looks
like he could grab his ankles

and roll like a donut. Not funny—
his chainsaw touched a whole world
of yellow jackets. They storm behind.

Each burst breath, a cry, a sting.
When Old Man reaches the truck,
he falls, bedeviled.

I tell Little Bother: "Roll him!"
We smother hornets in the dust.
We unfold the tarp

we carry to cover a load,
ger him wrapped in it, boost him
to the half-loaded bed.

"Got to get home. I drive!"
I yell, move the seat forward
so I can reach the clutch.

We lurch onto the road.
The bundled form breathes hard.
We need to get help.

The flare in the day blurs
time and event. I stop at a house
near the head of the creek.

They call, an ambulance comes.
Brother and I ride with this face,
swollen and calm. We are afraid.

I reach to grasp his hand,
to keep it from flopping off
the stretcher, his eyes puffed shut.

They give him a shot,
keep oxygen ready. They say
he'll live to tell about this.

All the way to Bay Hospital
I keep hold of his hand,
large, rough, and still.

DEAR TEACHER,

My report on Willamette
tributaries will not be done on
time.
This weekend I meant to
write it.
My father had a run-in
with yellow jackets. I spent Sunday
with him in the hospital.
I hope the delay will be excused
and it will nor lower my grade.
Sincerely,
Clete Hanks

CONFIDENCES

Clete tells his mother how
the Old Man rested his hand

in his: "I held it tighter
than he held mine. He kept
muttering, 'How sweet it is
to know you. How kind you are.'
Who was he talking to?
It wasn't me." Clete's mother:
"Does it matter? We like
calling him Wrench because
of his strength, yet he falls
in love at the drop of a hand-
kerchief. He's had dozens
of crushes. Whatever he said,
he said it to you."

Clete remembers to tell her
about the round that rolled
out of control, skipping
toward the pickup, gaining
speed, and at the road
with a little English
spun off the hill.
"It came this close!"

Conspiring, jocular, Clete
moves close to his mother.
"Remember last summer when

we camped at the burn?
I walked along the road,
up where white snags
stood stripped of their limbs.
Fallen trees had pried loose
bushel-sized rocks.

"I decided to see
how rocks roll through
a stand of snags,
like bowling. So I chose
a rock, nor the biggest,
but at first I couldn't roll it
out of its socket.
I pushed harder, tipped
it onto the slope, and
shoving with both feet
started it on its run.
I never told this to anyone.

"Head over heels it spun,
tripped on a downed tree,
hopped and sailed in the air,
going straight for a snag.
It struck with a thud,
seemed to pass right through.
The dead tree's top half
hung suspended for a moment,
then dropped with a crash.

"Now Father's hand in mine.
Dumb luck. Will there be
times like these again?"

"If it was dumb luck,
as you say, then, yes,
any day, any day."

WHERE OLD CARS FELL

On a roller-coaster gravel road
we approach where old cars fell.
I wonder if there's a summit,
a landing with a sweeping view,
a dizzy drop-off straight into
timber with enough crown
to swallow what is pushed
over the rim and down.
I ask my father how the cars
get here if they are really trashed.
Why go this far to dump a car
when junkyards on 101 pay for scrap?

"There's a boy in every man,"
he replies. "He wants to see
what happens, simple physics.
Wouldn't you push a rock
off trail just see it roll?
Fire's like that, starting
something, then losing control.
So's brawling, not caring
who wins or loses or gets hurt,
going with it, sure to break loose.

"I pity the rangers who
scramble down there
to figure how to get those cars.
They hire some stiff like me
from the woods, used to
heavy equipment, a gypo

with hooks and cables and
a rig big enough to reel stuff in.

"It's dicey grappling
a car body bumping rocks,
swinging out into midair,
inching right to the lip
of this landing where it could
catch or slip. It has to be
coaxed over the edge just so.
Imagine making a bid
on hooking several junkers
in thick brush, eighty feet down.
That guy needs a poker soul!"

BURN BARREL

A father named Wrench
teaches his sons this:

It's force, quick or slow,
mean, thoughtless, natural.

For sure, meanness.
Some don't think before

they shoot, drive too fast
along the slough, gig frogs.

Force, too, at the heart of the forest.
Stupendous growth of trees.

Sudden fires to claw them,
wind-whipped crown to crown.
And saws stutter and whine,
single-minded equalizers.

Soon gangs of fireweed rove clearcuts,
gullies scraped by winter gushers—

you can hear stones butting heads.

*

Clete wonders what the rest of the world
does for thought if they don't stand

by a burn barrel, watching
fames lick up the week's trash.

Do they get our squint-eyed stare,
our knack for following smoke?

This barrel is my school.

A BOY'S EYES

Now you understand.

In mind, Clete's and mine,
the gist of our story
is father-mother-son.
Clete dreams, observes,
finds his words. I write.
Together, we tease it out.

Fast on the slough road,
those whose hands grip
beer cans, given the luck,
given chance upon chance,
something fine turns up—
comfort in a glance or touch,
a sudden shut-up to the banter,
a knowing squint at
the mill-streaked sky,
afternoon fog raking
the eye of the sun.

A boy's eyes haze over
like the bay at three o'clock,
weary of staring at fire in the barrel
and swirling, bitter smoke.

Clete turns to his father,
who stands beside him near the rim.
Clete turns to his father and speaks . . .

THREE NOTES

The line about the saw touching a yellow jacket nest is drawn from Michael McGriff's poem "Mercy, Tear It Down."
One epithet for Clete's father—Buck Roller—was Scott Landfield's crew boss moniker when planting trees.
What I have experienced of rock rolling and busting snags comes from my work on trails with Ron Robinson and the Scorpions.

APPRECIATION

Toni Hanner's notice of "Several Winds," an earlier Coos poem published in For All I Know, *motivated me to go forward from "Clete says . . ." the first line, the first name.*
The readers of drafts—Tim Applegate, Mike Duran, Michael McGriff, Carter McKenzie, Ann Muller—supported this poem and suggested good changes.
*

As THREE NOTES *and* APPRECIATION *indicate, writing poetry occurs within a community.*

Carter McKenzie

A BRUTAL THEORY OF
THE FETAL HEARTBEAT

—after the overturning of Roe v. Wade
   by the Supreme Court Justices, June 24, 2022,
     following the expansion of the Second Amendment
      by the Supreme Court Justices, June 23, 2022

what is life inside
the girl or the woman
alive in her body

her depths these laws
presume, newly revived

the scrutiny of judges, remote
in their black robes, the majority
including one woman

making history

in backwardness

their obsession about who
rules the uterus, the blood cycle
of women and girls

the sanctity of life

the blood of abortion sickening them so much more
than death by the violence

they have just facilitated—

the day before, mulling over language

to expand the right to bear arms
of all kinds, the Second Amendment
having been treated

as if it were a *second-class right*

needing correction
no matter mass murder
after mass murder—

no matter Uvalde
the lives of children

not the point—

as is the case today, efficiently

clearing the way
for prosecutors

to track the records of women and girls
to track each and every abortion

against the encoded

baby of the law

of unreason

the baby and mother both

reduced
to detection

of a heartbeat, bodies
owned by the law

historic, written out

against the girl or woman
alive inside her body

the trees full
vital
in and of themselves

her own

these judges' argument against her

their dismissal:

it is none of her business
to decide, to conceive
or not

and how they rope

these laws around her life, a life
they cannot imagine
yet they proceed

they in fact would
they in fact do

let her burn

stacking the laws
like wood around her feet
tying her hands

ready to let the fire catch

CALLING FOR HIS MOTHER

—in memory of George Floyd

Calling for his mother

is a natural instinct
is the first instinct

when in danger

I have heard of this call
when bears
were eating a person alive
the bears unknowing

awful in their hunger
no word for it

indifferent, the story

bringing me

to my knees, fear in the vastness
of other beings

a humbling

my life unknown to them
how we are alone

a natural truth

I will be subject to but

what I cannot live with

what I say
I will not live with but I do

is the empty gaze of a white man

killing a Black man

beneath the weight
of the white man's knee

for nearly 10 minutes, other
officers watching

doing nothing
and as a white mother

I either live with that
or not, the absence

of good, a good man's soul

departing in our midst
on video, regular onlookers

pleading to lift

the unjust weight

crushing
deliberate
mindless

claim to law

and as a mother

I choose the bear

I wish upon the empty gaze
of the white man's system
the full
transformative

attention
of the bear

Note: Grateful acknowledgement to artist Kathleen Caprario for featuring "Calling for His Mother" in her mixed-media art installation interrogating the intersections of art, race, and privilege for the exhibition Social Being at Maude Kerns Art Center in 2022.

ON THE LAM

Tom A. Titus

A lacy accumulation of dirt and spider webs around my third-floor window framed a shimmering sun suspended in a camas sky. At lunch hour on this wide-eyed midsummer day, dwarf shadows crept hesitantly from shrubs in the courtyard below. Sunlight shattered into leaf-broke shade beneath a row of ornamental trees along 13th Avenue. The world outside seemed hell-bent on expanding beyond my reach.

I rarely buy lunch. Instead, I break away for a run. Return to my desk. Eat some culinary memory from the evening before that has been reanimated in a microwave. On this azure afternoon, I did not run and did not bring my lunch. I badly needed a dose of honest-to-god sunlight to offset the tinny fluorescence that illuminates the genetics lab where I squint away my daylight hours. I felt like a bookstore clerk squeezed into a dark aisle, suffocated by shelves bulging with literary profusion. Maybe I was short on sleep or hungry or tired of running from myself. Or maybe the answer was "all of the above." Underlying causes be damned, I was desperate for liberation.

Slamming through a side door of the biology complex clearly marked emergency exit, I crossed the street to the student union. The lunch hour line was full of people forty years younger. I ordered a full-size submarine sandwich with spinach and tomatoes and olives and pickles and goopy pink chipotle sauce. Emerging back into the broad arms of early afternoon, I headed for a bench in a courtyard outside my building, looking for a little space, a little peace, a little quiet.

Instead, all hell broke loose. There was nothing spectacular about this peculiar version of hell. It was only the daily brimstone most of us face down before staggering onward with our lives. The street was getting a facelift, and the surgical tool of the moment was a jackhammer. A jackhammer is not an instrument of quietude. The clatter of asphalt being reduced into black Cracker Jacks pierced my thin shield of fortitude, punched into my core, and began chiseling away at my personal bedrock.

Clutching my unwrapped sandwich, I fled. Surely small pieces of dismantled soul were being strewn behind. The campus crows would sweep in to gobble the bits of me, and I would become a noontime Hansel with no hope of return. My sanity was in jeopardy but remained intact as I moved resolutely through a grassy courtyard, powerwalking past tall brick buildings and several empty benches far too close to the jackhammers to serve as refuge. There would be another place far from the heartrending racket.

The construction noise faded when I emerged beside the broad and busy thoroughfare of Franklin Boulevard. No one knows for sure, but everyone thinks this short section of Pacific Highway *was* named for the spectacled, frugal, entrepreneurial patriot. A sunny hideaway beckoned beyond six lanes of cars and trucks converting my children's petroleum inheritance into an exhaust-spewing roar. I teetered at the edge of this noisy maw, on the verge of being devoured by the masticating stream of traffic. What would old Ben have thought seeing me standing at that curb, approaching something akin to agoraphobic panic, waiting to cross his chaotic namesake without the benefit of a crosswalk? Might he have told me that this is the nature of progress?

A small gap opened in the eardrum rupture of traffic. I darted through like a nocturnal deer mouse caught in the dazzling vastness of daylight.

Immediately beyond Franklin Boulevard, a footbridge spanned the Millrace. This lethargic filament of water was originally diverted from the Willamette River to drive hydro-powered industry in the late 1800s. Now the canal flows in placid neglect, walled in by impenetrable blackberry brambles sporting five-petaled white blossoms. A few finger-length fish twitched past a drowned bicycle resting on the muddy bottom. Perhaps the fingerlings wondered how they had come to live in such dishonorable circumstances. At least the water didn't stink.

Just past the footbridge was a small brick plaza with a south-facing concrete bench. A seemingly serene space to bathe my face under the high-flying sun. I propped myself against the expansive backrest and began to unwrap the submarine sandwich. But the bedlam from Franklin Boulevard wrapped around me like an octopus enveloping a crab, chewing away at my center. On any other day, the noise would have been tolerable. But on this day I was beaten down by the blare. Compelled to escape, I rewrapped the sandwich and fled further along the bike path, ever more desperate for that place with a little space, a little peace, a little quiet.

The path arrowed alongside a shady research park rife with straight edges: unreasonably tidy brick buildings, picnic tables on rectangular concrete pads, and manicured lawns ripe with the smell of irrigated grass. A tranquil scene of right angles: vertical, horizontal, perpendicular, all well-ordered and *intensely* respectable. Still too close to the blare of traffic. I didn't bother to stop.

My route ducked through an underpass beneath the railroad tracks. A dirt two-track road diverged from the asphalt to my right and was blocked by an iron gate sporting a no trespassing sign. I slowed down only enough to duck beneath it. Beyond the gate sprawled an interstitial space between the tracks and the Willamette River. The place held a roughshod air of defiance; it remained wholly incompatible with the intentions of developers who would plant buildings and pave the grass with parking lots. This was not a dysfunctional place. It simply had no function that served particular human needs. Weeds, wild grasses, and blackberries grew in tangled shelters for other-than-human beings: song sparrows, Oregon voles, and brush rabbits. It was only a happy accident that a frazzled biologist looking for a peaceful place to eat a well-traveled and rapidly warming submarine sandwich could find refuge here. In a sunny spot behind a bramble pile I planted my ass on a cast-off piece of railroad tie smelling of black creosote. Traffic noise dimmed. I began to peel the crinkly wrapper from the sandwich. Began to relax.

A train roared in. This was no stubby, pug dog train with an engine and a few cars flitting by. This was a full-on freight train. Seven engines pulled and pushed a jillion flatbed cars stacked with the blonde two-by-four remains of a forest now destined for a two-by-four store near you. A tooth-rattling clatter of iron wheels underscored the higher-pitched clank of cars jostling against their couplers. Each rolling stack of lumber seemed to be straining away from those monotonous tracks, striving to be liberated from an ignominious straight-line existence of enforced following. I recognized their predicament. But today the head-banging calamity of their struggle was unbearable. I couldn't be anything but self-absorbed and focused on protecting the meager remains of my noise-shattered soul and that godforsaken submarine sandwich. I kept traveling.

The riverbank was my last chance. In desperation, I ducked into a narrow trail forged through an otherwise impenetrable mountain of blackberry vines. The path dropped over a precipice of large rocks piled by people striving to shackle the innate tendencies of free-flowing water. The Willamette River was once a magnificent network of meandering and ever-changing channels. Winter and spring floods deposited fertile layers of pulverized mountains across the valley floor. The river did all this without regard to human needs, only because this is what an uninhibited river in a flat valley *does*.

The Kalapuya were fully integrated into this seasonal ebb and flow of the *Whilamut*. But new people rolled in and began growing food and planting houses on the loamy soil. They required control over those unfettered channels. The river was dammed, ditched, diked. Now the water molecules chase themselves in another ignominious straight-line existence of enforced following.

I picked my way to the foot of the rocky revetment. Between lapping water and drooping alder stretched a narrow band of respite. For a stool, I found a basketball-sized piece of gray basalt dislodged from a nameless outcrop far upstream in the Cascade Mountains. Sharp edges were worn smooth by its tumbling trip downriver. For millennia the stone had registered the music of water. Whispering current. Goose talk. Trilling frogs. The soft clicking of small pebbles made by salmon swishing nests in spawning gravel. Like me, the rock was on the lam, but for eons rather than an hour.

Here, I cowered, a panting fox running from the baying hounds of the built world. I unwrapped my beat-up submarine sandwich. Unwrapped the gauze protecting my innermost insides. Exposed brittle anxiety to the softening wash of river song rising from the gentle current. And from beneath me there rose a little space, a little peace, a little quiet. A murmuring memory of stone.

Jorah LaFleur

I WRITE

a spoken word poem

I write because there's a tiny world inside my every cell
and each has a story to tell

I write to be honest with myself

I write like my own secretary taking dictation,
recording and supporting, ongoing conversations

I write so that I might wander through decrepit casteless
marveling at the flowering vines, spontaneous lines
that grow to crumble stone walls

I write so that all the dams might be broken,
secret fears spoken in the company of strangers

I write to honor the anger

I write seething with love and drenched in fury

I write in a leisurely hurry, slow and deliberately rushing like a river,
I write to deliver floating bottle messages to my compass keeper lost at sea

I write to quell the endless swells of anxiety
I write to know the squeamish ache of embarrassment

I write to leach latent meaning from rhyme

I write to defy time —
to open the immortal portal and lick the lap of infinity

I write to taste divinity in art

I write to fight the fear of heart-revealing
ink-drip my feelings into your ears
that you might hear the sound of its pounding . . .

And, I write because You write
You, the Great Poets revered and famed,
You, the unnamed, the never remembered
You who play with what you say,
metaforcefully making way for new understandings
You who came before me
You who ignore me, or simply have no idea I'm listening

You

I write because You write
and your words are like a blood transfusion
slowly winding their way inside me
until muddled and mingled
into a single
pulse
your voice and my body
beat out their rhythms together
sometimes slow and melodic,
other times fast and frantic
like a winged animal caged,
sometimes enraged and insistent,
sometimes broken, halting, hesitant . . .

. . . and perhaps it is at these times
that I love You most purely,
when your hands betray you,
as you stand on stage paper shaking,
the every tremble of your modern parchment
ripples through me
and I am truly
in awe of the courage you've shown

I write so that You
might know you're not alone .
and I might know the same

ESCAPES

Nina Kiriki Hoffman

"Where are the books where you write your own ending?" the girl asked me. She was pale and bedraggled; her shoes were scuffed, and so was her face. The shoulders of her long brown coat were sopping from the rain outside the two-story building that housed Brannigan's Books. The brown leather satchel strapped across her chest bulged at her side, its clasps broken and outside pockets gaping to display a selection of her underwear, mostly white cotton. I wondered if I should ask her to check her bag. I didn't think she could shove anything else into it, even if she *wanted* to shoplift.

"The *Choose Your Own Adventure* books?" I glanced toward the kids' section. *Choose Your Own Adventure* books were from my childhood. I didn't know if anyone published them anymore. I'd only been working at Brannigan's for a week, and I didn't know the stock yet. Every time I straightened a section, I found all kinds of books I'd never heard of in my previous incarnation as a bookseller at a big chain store in Seattle.

David, the supervisor on duty, handed a little old lady a copy of the latest *Witches' Almanac* and came to the cash wrap. "Hey, Sylvia, need some help?" he asked.

Everybody at Brannigan's was really nice. They didn't trust me yet. Every time I tried to answer a customer's question, somebody swooped up and checked on me, which was probably a good thing, as I usually had the wrong answer, apparently. It was as if my eight years in book sales didn't mean a thing.

They were watching me as though I was a baby chick in a hen yard. It was nice. It was also driving me nuts.

I needed this job. I couldn't go back to Seattle. Peter was there, terrifyingly there, with all his friends, not all of whom I knew, but all of whom knew about me. The three earlier times I had tried to escape, Peter had tracked me down with the help of his watchful friends, and then he punished me for abandoning him. Those times, I hadn't left town, just moved to new apartments in different suburbs. To escape, I had to leave everything behind, change my name, my hair color, my behavior. I still wasn't sure I was safe, but at least I was somewhere else.

I liked my new town, Tonkit, somewhere in the middle of Washington State, not on any direct route from Seattle to anywhere else. So it was small, and I was lonely; at least I had my own place. I could go home without worrying that Peter would be waiting in the apartment for me with another suitcase full of things he called toys.

Well, that wasn't true. I always worried. The change was that even though I worried, nobody was there when I got home, and the tension that twisted my guts relaxed a little more every night.

I loved selling books. Books had saved my life time after time when I was a teenager and there was no way I could leave home except by reading. Hell, they had helped me survive the time I spent with Peter. I got a rush helping other people find the perfect escape.

I was lucky Brannigan's hired me. It was the only bookstore in town, and not an easy place to get a job. Some of the clerks had been there fifty years. Nobody ever quit unless they were moving or they died. I'd seen the tall stack of applications the owner had received. My application was good, even though the references were fake. But I had been lucky too, or maybe my interview went really well. I still wondered why I had gotten the job, but I surely didn't want to lose it. I was still on probation to see how I worked out.

I could survive being helped too much.

"I'm looking for the books where you write your own ending," the soggy girl said in a soft voice to David.

"Ah," said David. "Follow me." He didn't head for the kids' section, but back into the stacks where new and used books rubbed shoulders, and parts of each section were set up based on the special knowledge of the clerks. Elizabeth, the owner, had asked me after I was hired what I had special knowledge of, and she'd set up a shelf just for me. "Stock all your favorites here," she said, "the books you can sell because you've read and loved them." So far I'd ordered a hiking guide, three plant identification books, my favorite biography of Houdini, an illustrated book about the goddesses of India, three historic mysteries, four kids' books, and eight fantasy novels.

Miki, another clerk, was nearby, talking to the bookstore cat, Tetisheri. "Watch the front?" I asked her.

"Sure."

I followed David and the customer. I wanted to know where everything was, and I hadn't heard of this book category before.

Against the back wall between the sections on Self-Help and History, there was a bookshelf I hadn't noticed, with a fold-down desk and a collapsible metal chair below it. The books on the shelf were covered in various fabric colors and designs, and none of them had titles.

"What kind of story is it?" David asked the soggy girl.

"It's about a runaway."

David *tsked* his tongue against the roof of his mouth, scanned the book spines. He picked one covered in faded blue denim, opened it, skimmed a couple of pages, and handed it to the girl.

She turned to the first page. She read a paragraph, then glanced up at David. Her smile was like a shaft of sunlight coming through a cloud. "Thank you."

He held the chair for her. She sat at the desk, the book open in front of her. He handed her a pen.

"Thank you," she whispered again, her gaze already fixed on the words. David nodded, then took my arm and led me back to the cash wrap.

"She's going to write in that book?" I asked. "A book she hasn't even paid for?"

"She'll pay later."

"That's a category? Books where you write your own ending?"

David smiled. He was an older man, slight and wispy, with iron-framed glasses and a retreating hairline. He dressed in blues and grays, soft sweatery shirts and vests and nondescript slacks. He had a V-shaped smile that changed him from invisible into something cunning, sparkly, and almost dangerous. I had been trying to train myself not to back away when he smiled, but I still stepped back. His smile widened. "We have special customers for that section. Let me know if anybody else asks. It takes a while to learn those books."

"Okay."

I was helping a kid track down a book about dragon hunting—Miki told me to check Juvenile Non-fiction—when the soggy girl emerged from the stacks.

Her clothes had changed: her full-length coat was lavender and waterproof now; her leather satchel had changed into a big black suitcase with wheels, and clasps that held it shut; her scuffed shoes had turned into elegant high-button boots. Her face had filled out. She smiled as she paid David, using a shiny new credit card.

Okay, my only clue that she was the soggy girl was that she was buying the denim-covered book. I took a couple steps toward the cash wrap, longing for a better look at her, but the boy tugged on my arm.

"They don't have a picture of the dragon I want," he said, waving the *Illustrated Guide to Dragons* at me.

I knelt beside him and helped him look through the descriptions of the dragons. He was right; there was no black and gold dragon the size of a baseball in the book.

This was Brannigan's, so I checked the shelf again, and found two more large books with full-color illustrations. We searched them and finally found the information he wanted. He read it carefully. He asked me how much the book cost.

"Thirty dollars," I said.

His face turned red. "I've only got three bucks," he mumbled.

"That's okay."

I rose and re-shelved the books. "I bet this book will be here when you come back, if you still want it. Want to find something else today?"

He bought a used paperback about mummies. By that time, the soggy girl was gone.

On my mid-afternoon break I went into the back office where we did the bookkeeping, kept the overstock, and received new books. It was a dark, cavernous room with shelves up to the ceiling on every wall and no windows. It had a dark pink carpet that reminded me unpleasantly of the surface of a tongue.

Piranella, the store's used book buyer, had her own desk there where she repaired used books, covered them with mylar dust jackets, and priced them. The rest of us sat at Elizabeth's desk when we were on break, below the small oil portrait of the store's founder, her great-grandfather Samuel Brannigan. Her desk was an antique monster with lots of drawers in it, most of them locked. We were all taught the combination to her file drawer, where the female clerks kept their purses during their shifts.

Miki was in the back room, sorting new receiving into categories on three rolling carts.

I got my lunch bag and the current book I was reading out of the tote bag I had brought. I settled to eat at Elizabeth's desk. "How long have you worked here?" I asked Miki.

"Six years."

"No kidding? How old are you?" She looked about sixteen, though she was Japanese, so it was hard for me to judge.

"Twenty-four," she said.

"Wow. So do you know every section in the store yet?"

Miki laughed. "Nobody knows every section. Don't let them fool you. Yesterday I saw Clifton find a shelf he'd never seen before."

"Gosh." Clifton was the senior clerk. He'd been at the store for fifty-three years, longer than Elizabeth had owned it. "What was on it?"

"A full set of encyclopedias from 1879. Just what somebody was looking for. A dollar a volume for a set of twenty-four. They'd been there so long we don't even know who priced them; maybe they'd been there since they were published."

"Did you know they were there?"

"I'd seen them before. I'm the only one who uses a duster, remember? I've touched more books in this store than anybody else, I bet."

"I just saw David show somebody a section of books where you write your own ending. Do you know about those?"

The tip of Miki's tongue stuck out of her mouth. She took a stack of books out of a box and stuck them on the New Age section of the cart. "I've seen people shop that section once in a while. I get the wanders when I head there."

"The wanders."

Her black eyes glanced at me, then away. "You know. When the store pushes you another direction?"

"Um?"

"You haven't gotten the wanders yet? Relax. They'll come. It's very helpful. When I've forgotten where something is, I get these little nudges from the store. Listen to your feet. The floor's telling them where to go. You'll wind up in front of the right shelf."

"The wanders." I opened my yogurt and stirred the fruit.

"Or maybe you won't get them." Miki shrugged and opened another box.

"I'd like to. Sounds helpful. I just never had them at my other store."

"Your other store." Another shrug.

I ate my yogurt and banana and let the conversation wilt, the way my shoulders were doing. I guessed everyone who worked at independent bookstores hated the chains. I'd heard stories about how the big chain bookstores drove little stores out of business, built big stores in locations specifically to kill little stores. It hadn't happened in Tonkit, of course. Tonkit was too small. In fact, it was surprising that Brannigan's survived. We were close enough to draw Canadian book buyers over the border, and even though Tonkit wasn't on any tourist route, we seemed to pull in a lot of out-of-towners. The first day I worked here I had talked to people from Paris, Tokyo, and Cairo. Each had found books in their own language, too. I wasn't sure how I would straighten the foreign language sections if they were ever assigned to me. How do you alphabetize Arabic when you can't even read it?

I checked my watch. My fifteen-minute break was up. I disposed of my trash, put my book in my tote bag, and headed back to work.

For a minute there, I'd thought maybe Miki and I were making friends, and I'd felt hopeful. Sure would be nice to have somebody to rent videos with (Tonkit was too small to have a movie theater). Microwave popcorn was as haute as my cuisine usually got. I seemed to have somehow soured my chances for friendship though.

Just before I crossed the threshold between the office and the store, the pink rug rose up and licked my leg just above my hiking boot and below the cuff of my black jeans. I stumbled out the door into the wood-floored store, slipped, and fell on my seat.

I glanced over my shoulder at the rug.

Perfectly flat, totally quiescent.

The wide black door shut. The lock clicked. Had Miki followed me to the door and locked me out? I had the office keys; all the employees did. Maybe she was making some kind of point. Whatever it was, I didn't get it.

"Are you all right, Sylvia?" David held out a hand and helped me to my feet.

"You ever get the feeling the office is a great big mouth?"

"Of course, but it never swallows, only tastes. Would you like to straighten the Self-Help section this afternoon?"

"Love to," I said.

Self-Help was back by the shelf where the soggy girl had been. When I got there, the desk was folded up into the wall; the chair had been collapsed and slid into a little alcove just the right size to shelter it. No wonder I'd never noticed the desk before. I reached for one of the fabric-covered books. They were part of our inventory, and I wanted to know more about them. There was a turquoise one that particularly intrigued me. Before I touched it, though, I turned around and headed for the beginning of my section.

I spent two hours alphabetizing by author as hard as I ever had. By the time I'd reached Wegscheider-Cruse / Williamson / Zukav, my shift was over.

When I went to the office to collect my purse, tote bag, and jacket, I noticed two things: the office was warmer than the rest of the store, and the air smelled faintly of peppermint. Miki had finished all the receiving and was out in the store somewhere, shelving new books. I hesitated before I went to the computer to clock out.

The room acted like a room.

I logged off, got my belongings, and stood in front of the door for a moment.

Then I turned and went to the corner past the safe and the file cabinet, where there was a little alcove. I dropped my things and sat down, placed my palms flat on the furry pink rug. It felt rough but not wet.

"Well," I said.

I stroked my hand across the ridged and nubbly carpet. I leaned against the wall. I patted the carpet again. I thought I felt a faint vibration under my hands, a distant purr.

I was imagining things.

My imagination was the best friend I had.

"Guess I should go home," I muttered.

It wouldn't be as warm at home, of course, and I would have to do what I did every evening: stand in front of my apartment door while my stomach tied itself in knots, steel myself to unlock the door, go in and look around, gripping the blackjack I bought before I left Seattle. I had no idea if I could actually use it on another human being. After a check of the apartment, I would settle down with the current book, fix a little dinner and a big pot of tea, read, maybe, all alone . . .

My eyes drifted shut. I slid down, curled up there with my cheek against the rug. The store was open until eleven p.m. and it was only seven now. Nobody would mind if I—

"You don't mind if I nap here?" I asked Samuel Brannigan. He was a sturdy man in old-fashioned clothes. He had wild red hair parted in the middle, and elegant handlebar mustaches. His eyes were bright blue, his cheeks ruddy.

"Not at all. All part of the process. Bit sooner than usual, though."

"I'm so lonely."

"They all are when they first arrive, Lexi. Don't mind if I call you that, do you? Sylvia's just not right."

I laughed. Then I sobered. "But you won't call me that in the waking world, will you?"

"Couldn't if I would, Love. I'm not in the waking world. I died quite a while back."

"Not all the way, huh?"

He laughed. "That's right. The body's gone, but there's lots of me left. How do you like my establishment?" He held his arms out and looked around the room. The walls melted and we saw through them into the store, where books hung in the air on invisible shelves, each one alive with stories and information, gifts and salvation, waiting to help.

"I love it," I whispered.

"Are you in this business for life?"

"That would be my dream come true."

He stared at me. He took my hands and peered into my eyes. "Give us a kiss, then."

I'd never kissed a ghost before. Oh well. It had to be better than kissing Peter. I stood on tiptoe, and aimed my lips at his. He put his arms around me and pulled me up against him. His kiss was gentle, searching.

After a long time, he lifted his head. "You're a strange lass, Lexi."

"Too strange?" My heart thudded. Had I done something wrong here too, and soured all my chances again?

"Oh, no. No! Don't worry, Love. We'll keep you on."

I kissed his hand.

"Sylvia? Sylvia, wake up. What are you doing still here?"

I rubbed my cheek against Brannigan's shirt, which felt rougher and scratchier than it had looked.

I opened my eyes, looking up into David's face. "I'm sorry. I fell asleep."

"Strange. You've only been here a week."

"I know." I sat up and yawned against the back of my hand.

"You're still in the first stage of the review process. Er—or maybe you were just tired?"

"That's right." I stroked my cheek. Rug burn. "Please don't fire me."

I flinched.

A book had dropped from a high shelf to land open beside my hiking boot.

David and I leaned forward.

You're not going anywhere, said the first line on the page.

"Oh," I said. "All right. Thanks."

"Hmm. I guess the review period is over. Won't be official until Liz says it is, but welcome to Brannigan's, Sylvia." David chewed on the first knuckle of his index finger. "Are you going to spend the night?"

"I don't know." My stomach growled. There was a bathroom, of course, with lots of bookseller humor on the walls, but there was no shower that I knew of, and I didn't have any more food with me. Still, I would spend the night if I was supposed to.

Pages of the book flipped. They stopped. Go home, said the line at the top of the page.

"Okay. Thanks." I blew the carpet a kiss and stood up.

"You worked at one of the big chains before," David said.

"Yes."

He shook his head. "Surprising. Of course, your references didn't check out, but nobody's ever do. See you tomorrow."

"Yes. Good night." I left David to his bookkeeping and headed out through the dark and silent store. I trailed a hand along the bookshelves, touching something more than wood, paper, cloth spines and leather. I made it to the front door without tripping over anything and paused to stare out at my new town through the glass.

Rain drifted down, slicking the pavement of Main Street and capturing puddles of reflected light from the few signs lit at eleven at night: next door, Daylight Doughnuts' sign was on; they stayed open until two a.m. Across the street, the sign for Mabel's Diner was dark. At Tucker's Tavern next door, beer-logo neon flickered in the small high windows, sparking colors from the water on the street. The door to Tucker's opened and someone staggered out.

I gripped the door handle and turned it. Time to go home. Tomorrow ought to be different. I could ask them to call me Lexi now, maybe.

My apartment was only a block away from Brannigan's, upstairs from the Greasy Spoon, a tiny cafe with only a counter, no tables. Kash, the breakfast cook, served the best home fries I'd ever eaten. I had them every morning.

I climbed the outside staircase, reached into my tote for the blackjack, running on automatic. I felt sleepy and jubilant. It didn't matter whether Miki liked me; the store had chosen me. I had a future now.

I gripped the blackjack and opened my front door.

Peter grabbed my arm before I could raise it, twisted my wrist until I had to drop my weapon, pulled my arm up behind my back until it screamed with pain. He dropped my arm and snapped something around my neck before I could catch my breath.

"Hey, Lexi," he said in his purring voice, the one that stroked you like a feather. "You're supposed to get home at seven-ten. Why are you so late?"

My right arm felt like it had been torn off. I checked. It was still attached.

I walked into my apartment and dropped my tote bag, then lifted my left hand to the collar he'd put on me.

"Want to see how it works?" he asked.

"No," I whispered. It *worked?* It wasn't just a humiliating fashion statement.

Well, of course it worked. This was Peter.

"You need to know."

I turned toward him. Fire shot through my neck. It felt like I had been decapitated, only the pain went on and on. When it was over, I found myself curled up on the floor.

"Sit on the couch, Lexi. Don't be such a slob."

My muscles still worked, though they were spasming. I levered myself up and went to the couch.

Peter held a remote control. His familiar suitcase lay on the coffee table in front of the couch. He came and sat beside me, took my hand, played with my fingers. "Shall we talk about how frustrated I am?"

"Anything you want." My voice was back to its old monotone, though a little harsh.

"You were very hard to find this time. I had to pay strangers for information."

"Why. . ." I whispered.

His finger hovered over the red button on the remote, then dropped to the side. "Go ahead. Ask."

"Why did you follow me? Why did you find me? Why won't you let me go?"

"I love you, Lexi. There's something so *perfect* about you. You're the best woman I've ever owned. It's like somebody built you just for me."

Yes. Father had done that. So much of what Peter enjoyed was similar to what Father had enjoyed. Living with Peter had felt familiar. Uncomfortably comfortable.

Then one day I read a book. It was a book I'd read before, but this time some of the words rose up off the page and pounded into my brain.

Sandy, the waitress at the coffee shop where I ate lunch, noticed which book I was reading, and said she had read it too. We talked every day for a while. She helped me pull my courage together enough to run away from Peter that first time.

"Besides, I can't let you get away," said Peter. "It sets a bad example for the others. They're watching me. They'll expect to see that I've punished you properly for all the trouble you've given me." He leaned forward and spun the combination lock on his suitcase, flipped the top up. He had added to his toy collection. "Hmm. What shall I start with? I know. Your favorite. Take off your shoes, darling."

"No," I whispered.

He touched the red button on the remote.

When I could see straight again, I took off my shoes.

"I have to say good-bye to my new boyfriend," I whispered the next morning. I had no voice left.

"A new boyfriend? I've had someone watching you for a while, and nobody mentioned that detail." Peter had packed everything he'd brought but the remote. He had only to move a finger and I would do whatever he wanted; he had trained me all night.

"He's at the bookstore."

"These workplace romances. So risky. Are you sure you want me to see this person? You know how jealous I am."

"I'll just leave a note."

"Wouldn't it be better to just leave? No. Now that I know, I have to see him. Who could you prefer to me?" He knelt at my feet, slid fresh socks up over my bloody soles, smiled as I winced. During the night I had packed everything I had acquired since I left Seattle. He opened one of my suitcases and took out a pair of moccasin slippers. "Or would you prefer your tennis shoes?"

I didn't say anything. I would prefer never to walk again.

Peter handed me a jacket. "Better put this on. Your forearms are a bit obvious. I'm glad I saved your face for later. Fresh bruises are more frightening to the others. Isn't that nice? Your new lover can see you and think you're still just fine."

He left me on the couch while he loaded his suitcase and mine into the trunk of his car, then returned to escort me downstairs.

Knives sliced into my feet with every step I took. The first steps were the worst. After a little I remembered old skills; I dialed down the intensity of pain and walked almost normally, with only a phantom wince each time I put my foot down.

"You're early, Sylvia," Elizabeth said when she saw me.

"I've come to quit," I whispered.

"You can't quit. David said you passed review."

"I'm sorry. I have to leave," I whispered.

She came out from behind the cash wrap. "Are you all right, my dear?" she asked. "You don't look well."

"My fiancée was just having a touch of wedding nerves," Peter said from behind me. "She ran off and led me a merry chase. Imagine. She can't stay here, ma'am. I need her back at home."

"Introduce me to your young man, Sylvia."

"Peter McIntosh, Elizabeth Brannigan. Elizabeth, this is Peter, the one I ran away from."

"I see," she said slowly.

The floor pulsed under my feet, sending fire through all the new sores. I cried out, only my gasp was ragged, torn from a voiceless throat.

"Lexi says she has to say good-bye to her new boyfriend," Peter said.

"Ah," said Elizabeth. "I'd like to give her a farewell present as well."

"What sort of present?" Peter asked.

"A book, of course." She darted away from us.

"Where's the sweetheart?" Peter asked me.

"In the office."

"Show me."

I took out my keys. Carefully I opened the key ring and pulled my office key off of it. I limped down the aisles past the shelves to the wide black door of the office. Peter followed me.

What could he do? What on earth did I imagine the ghost of Samuel Brannigan could do?

I could imagine lots of lovely things. My imagination was as far as events like that usually got.

I unlocked the door and flicked on the light. The room was just the way I had left it—no sign that David had sat at Elizabeth's desk crunching numbers and counting up the till.

"There's no one here," Peter said, staring in from the store.

"I'll leave a note." I stumbled to the desk and took a piece of stationery out of Elizabeth's middle drawer. *Dear Sam*, I wrote.

Peter came silently up behind me and leaned over to watch me write.

I have to leave now. I'm so sorry. All I want to do is stay here with you.

The pink carpet snapped up and around Peter. He screamed and dropped the remote. The carpet wrapped tighter until all that was visible of Peter was his head. A corner of the carpet stuffed itself into his mouth.

David came in and handed me a book bound in turquoise cloth. "From Elizabeth," he said. He glanced at Peter's head, then at the remote. "Hmm."

Peter stared at David, his eyes wide and angry.

I tugged at my collar. "Can you see how this comes off?" I leaned forward, pulling my hair in front of my shoulders.

David's cool fingers brushed the back of my neck. "It's not immediately obvious. Can it wait? I need to show you something."

I straightened.

"This is your book," David said. "You must write the ending. It works better if you dip your pen in blood. This is a blood sampler." He handed me what looked like a fat, angular pen, with a button and a slide on its side. "You cock it like this, and when you press the trigger, a lancet pops out of this tip and digs a hole in your finger. It's less painful if you lance the sides of your finger, up near the fingernails, rather than the fingertip. Understand?"

"I think so."

He laid a pen on the desk in front of me, patted my shoulder. "I'll leave you to it, then."

After he left, I opened the book to the front.

"Where are the books where you write your own ending?" the girl had asked me.

I flipped ahead to where the writing ended. The last sentence was, AFTER HE LEFT, I OPENED THE BOOK TO THE FRONT.

I thought for a little while. I glanced at Peter, whose face was so red I wondered if he'd die of suffocation or heart attack, releasing me from everything. Maybe Sam was killing him for me.

But that wasn't fair.

I lanced the middle finger of my left hand and dipped the pen into the upwelling blood. Then I wrote:

> *Lexi's father rose from the grave with only one mission in mind. After all he had done to his daughter, he needed to make amends. He needed to make her safe, to free her from all the things he had taught her.*
>
> *He stepped into the office—*

The hair on the back of my neck prickled. The room, which had been warm, cooled to the temperature of ice. I didn't turn around.

> *—went to Peter and picked him up. Peter was helpless to do anything in the father ghost's grasp. "Come on, son. I'd like to show you my basement," said Lexi's father.*

Even as I wrote, I heard the words being spoken beside me.

> *Lexi's father walked away through the wall, taking Peter with him. He did not stop until he reached the basement, which had neither windows nor doors but was full of all the toys Father had collected across the years. "Ah, my son," said Father. "I'm glad you're here. I have so much to teach you."*
>
> *Lexi never saw Peter or Father again. She lived happily ever after in Tonkit, working at Brannigan's Bookstore.*

I closed the book, set down the pen. When I looked up, Peter was gone. I lay down in the little alcove beyond the filing cabinet. I closed my eyes.

Samuel Brannigan smiled at me in my dream.

"Thank you," I said.

"Of course."

"You're not like them, are you?" Had I just exchanged my first two prisons for another?

"Only a little," he said. "And you can rewrite that part if you like."

I hugged him. He didn't smell at all like Father, or Peter for that matter; he smelled like pipe tobacco and bay rum and horses. "What did he do to your feet?" asked Samuel. His lips tasted my forehead for a long moment. "Great jumping Jehoshaphat. Holy leaping lords, Child!" He laid me down, then rushed off somewhere. . .

I opened my eyes sometime later to find David sitting on the carpet near me, my book open in his lap. He closed it and smiled at me. "Elizabeth's called the doctor. We'll take care of you."

I closed my eyes. It didn't stop the tears from leaking out.

"Hey, Lexi. Welcome home," said David.

Bob Craven

ODE TO A DOG,
HIT BY A BEER TRUCK

surging beneath the old green truck,
his legs, his ears,
his eyes, his back, were knotted
and torn back apart;

teeth clang rear axle,
scrape,
bounce;
his faith broke
as he spun out behind;

the truck skimmed on bald tires;
his fur whirled up into the wind;
his fur gummed to the asphalt;

chassis imprints;
final thump over back right ankle;
bounce, stop,
stop;

softly
he rolled to one side,
cracked his neck:

burst of psycho-grooveshards
then blizzards;
then colorglares;
then lightneedles;
he felt pretty bad,

he felt as if in bed,

then
a transactional blast
and he was gone,
the love rain above him
pure red.

"ETERNAL MYSTERY"

a fishing poem

Mid-nineties Chevy
on the gravel shoulder.
Wet, dark road.

Fire, fish in the crash.
But quiet under the air.
Fat man in waders.
Keystone man in rubber pants.
Still as the sun,
he hovers over swift water.
Fire, fish in the crash.
The Chevy not far away.

Above the creek, his waxy ear;
a droplet hanging off the earlobe;
sweat; the smell of shit when it rains.
He fishes with dry hand on the rod.
It is not a new smell, but it reminds him
of newness—a snail's new shell;
not a new smell—a little new shape,
a turning flame, wrapped all up in cellophane.

String in mouth; rod between thighs;
net in armpit; freed up hands
collecting the fat sides of trout.

Cecelia Hagen

SHELL GAME

I don't want to aim for
wisdom in a poem, that's
dangerous, worse even
than a branch

that's broken and hanging loose,
an open upstairs window
with no screen, a girl
who walks on a dark street
at a dangerous hour
and refuses to go home.

Guessing games are my specialty,
though I lose when I play
with kids because I let them
win. Maybe I'm wrong

to behave this way--life
is only kind of
kind, only part
of the time. Still, what harm

in a little sweetness? But now
it sounds like wisdom
is wedging in, when all I really want
is to unscramble an egg,
scoop its wet jelly
back into the jagged
pieces of shell, then
reunite them, hold that smooth
perfection in my palm,
hand it over to someone.

CECELIA HAGEN

LOVE SONG FOR A LONG MARRIAGE

My twinkle lights hanging from
             your gutter of leaves.
My spiny stems,
         your silk flowers.

My crooked stack of books,
the open tome nestled in your lap.

My stars, your moon
suspended in a sunlit sky
like a shy
giant in a children's story.

My stars hidden then.

Your stretched-out sweatshirt, my box
             of buttons. Your rice,
my beans. Always,
             my beans.

You rise, I swirl.
I cinnamon, you sriracha
                 dance alone, not always
         alone.

The shadows
     slipping out of your pencil,
my ink spilling and stopping.

My cork bark, your smooth sides.
Your Alhambra, my wooden pew.

Your blood rage,
                 my blue.

EYE CONTACT

Valerie Ihsan

I know what it's like to have $16 in my checking account until the next payday. I know what it's like to call in a $20 debt from my best friend so I can fix my bike to ride it to work, because I don't have the money to buy gas to *drive* to work. I know what it's like to get a $25 overdraft charge for non-sufficient funds because the $2.99 Apple iCloud storage payment I forgot about auto-withdrew— followed by two more NSF charges the same weekend because of a check clearing I'd written two months prior for a medical bill, and an annual website auto-renewal. I've known the shame of standing in line for a food box as a single mother of two children because I made too much money for food stamps. I've often wondered where needed money would come from—even with a job and an entrepreneurial side hustle, or two.

But I've never known homelessness. Nor have I ever worried about it.

I have a large enough network of family and friends that I'll always have somewhere to go. There's always someone to catch my fall.

In my almost half-a-century of being alive, I've learned a few things about myself. One is I'm highly empathetic. Not like the empath Deanna Troi from *Star Trek: The Next Generation*, though I resonated with that character.

I can't know what you are feeling—even though sometimes that would be handy. Like the rest of humanity, I wonder what my spouse is thinking. I'm not telepathic. But, despite potentially risking the general population's opinion of me, I do *get a feeling.* I sense the vibe in the room. I read body language. I hear hesitation and observe things unsaid.

In an earlier career as a massage therapist, before each client, I'd go through a little just-for-me ritual of grounding myself and shielding. Otherwise, a client's emotions could catch me off guard and I'd start crying in the middle of giving someone a massage *for no reason of my own.* At the end of each session, I always washed my hands, symbolically cleansing myself of any residual energy from my client. So, when I see people in pain, I hurt.

When I know a fellow human is in despair, I feel it.

When I see an animal that's been tortured, or even thoughtlessly neglected, *I* feel their anguish and loss of hope. I see how it must've happened to them. It plays out in my mind like a movie scene.

And so I protect myself.

I have to.

I look away.

I hate that I avoid eye contact with people on the street corners asking for help. When I think of the courage they must have in order to stand in public, facing ridicule and rejection, I feel shame. If they can do that, why can't I even look at them? I ought to at least afford them the courtesy of a smile or a wave or a hello—especially if I don't have a dollar to give them.

One rainy morning, I dropped my kids off at school and began my errands at the grocery store, Market of Choice, on Willakenzie Road. I swung by the coffee counter first to get an Americano. When I turned to the adjacent counter to add half-and-half and sugar, I almost collided with a man doing the same.

"Oh! I'm sorry," I said, stepping back.

He gestured for me to go ahead of him. "I'm used to waiting," he said with a smile.

Upon closer inspection, I could tell by his clothing—tidy, but damp—and his things just outside the door, that he was most likely homeless.

"Please," I said, inviting him to go first.

After I'd doctored my coffee, I made eye contact with him.

"Have a good day, sir," I said with a nod.

I tell myself I avoid the haunted eyes of the unhoused for my own mental health protection. I can't take on their pain, their fear, their despair. Depression would swallow me whole and I'd never be able to function. Depression and anxiety have taunted me for years and I've learned some tools to keep them at bay. Journaling helps, as well as surrounding myself with positive people, and taking my vitamins and mood supplements. I use UV light therapy seven or eight months out of the year, and snuggle with my dogs multiple times a day. I try to stay as physically healthy as I can, I don't watch the news, and I avoid doomscrolling on social media. I give money to animal shelters; *#adoptdontshop;* and always try to be nonviolent in my communication, consumption, and output.

And sometimes, I make eye contact.

One crisp morning, my whole day upended because of a cardboard sign and the singular sadness of my young son.

The sign said, *Living in Truck, Need Dogfood.* My son was mortified, heartbroken that this man lived in his truck and that the beautiful black dog at his heels needed to eat. My son wept in the van on the way to school.

I promised him I would pick up some dog food and bring it back to the man before I went home.

"The man was so skinny, he'll probably eat some of that dog food, too," he said.

My heart swelled, and I almost choked.

As promised, after dropping my children both off, I swung around to Market of Choice and picked up some apples, bananas, and a small bag of dog food. I drove around for a half an hour trying to find him. He wasn't at the corner anymore.

I scanned the park under the bridge across the street from where Robert reported seeing him, and where a lot of homeless people lived and visited. *I think I see him.* I circuited up the bridge, off an exit, and back on the bridge three times before deciding that it most likely was him. But I was leery of walking into a group of, maybe twenty, homeless people. That was far different from handing something out of my window at a light.

So, I left.

Headed home.

Too afraid.

I got almost all the way there before *I knew with certainty* that there was no way I could pick up Robert at school that day and tell him I *didn't* help the man and his dog—and the groceries were in my car, reminding me I had failed. I turned around again and drove back over the bridge.

I parked across the street and carried the dog food and the bag of apples and bananas to the group of people. I didn't see a dog anywhere.

What am I going to say to these people?

A couple of them noticed me, one shielding his eyes from the morning sun as I advanced. I called out from about ten yards away.

"Were one of you guys on the corner with a dog earlier?" My heart pounded.

A series of *yeah*s followed and a sweetie of a dog (black Lab something) came out from the middle of the group.

"My son saw you and wanted me to bring you this." I held out the grocery bag and dog food.

"Aw, thank you."

"That's so good of you!"

"God bless you."

"That's sweet."

"I'm sorry there's not more of it," I said.

I shook someone's hand. Another offered me a free concert—he would play me his guitar. Another asked me to pray for him.

It felt good.

But that was almost thirteen years ago.

And I still avoid eye contact.

I still try not to drown in despair and feel too much.

I still succumb to self-hatred when I think, *Why am I putting myself above them? Why should I not despair when they do? Who am I to ignore the suffering of others?*

When I start gulping for air and look wildly about for any place for my eyes to land but on the despair in front of me, I recognize I've reached the tipping point. The trigger spot in the negative mind spiral where if I don't redirect *now*, abort *now*, things will get ugly up in my brain for a long time.

So, I do.

I abort and try not to hate myself for it. I abort when I need to and stretch myself when I can.

Like last year. Last year, I stretched.

One morning, I arrived at work—Tsunami Books—and discovered a young man sleeping in the parking lot. He was in a thick sleeping bag, his blond hair tousled out in the chilly air on a makeshift pillow, his rucksack.

My elbows locked up, and dread filled my interstitial spaces like wet, unset concrete. *What should I do?*

I usually avoid conflict of all kinds. Especially ones where justice is on no one's side and it is a no-win situation for everyone. Ones where my socioeconomic and racial privilege makes someone else's day shitty.

He was only sleeping. Hurting no one. I hated it was *illegal* to sleep in our city.

I didn't want him to get in trouble, but I couldn't have him there when customers started arriving, and then I cringed for even having that passing thought.

I took a deep breath, walked past him, and unlocked the door to the bookstore.

While I turned on lights, the heaters, and the computers, I thought of what to do. How could I safely and kindly approach him, wake him, and get him out of the parking lot in fifteen minutes?

Using my empathy, instead of shielding it this time, I actively sought out what he might feel upon waking.

He'd probably only been asleep for a few hours at most. He might have taken something to help him forget, to numb, or to stay warm, and waking up from that might be uncomfortable. He might feel embarrassed or afraid. I couldn't take any of that away, and I couldn't, sadly, allow him the one thing that temporarily could. Sleep.

I'd never woken up in a parking lot before, but I had woken up too early, under the influence of various intoxicants, not feeling my best. My hands stilled at their tasks. *I know what to do.*

I went next door to the coffee kiosk and bought a muffin and a large coffee. I walked around the side of the building and set down the coffee cup two feet away from the blond man's eyes, hoping it would be the first thing he saw. I set the muffin on the lid, like a crown. Squatting behind my offering, creamers and sugar packets in my palm, I called out in a calm voice.

"Hey."

My heart rate had slowed.

I had a plan, and it was a good one.

I was doing my job—opening the store and creating a welcoming environment for the customers—and I was allowing the man in front of me some dignity, showing him compassion.

I was making a small difference in someone's life. Someone who'd had a crappy night.

I was making eye contact.

"Good morning," I sing-songed quietly.

He blinked his eyes open and jerked his head, momentarily startled.

I smiled at him and pointed at the bookstore behind him.

"I work in there, and we're just about to open, so I'll need you to move on now."

He sat up and blinked again. Slow. Getting his bearings.

"I brought you a coffee and a muffin. Didn't know if you'd want these." I showed my hand of creamers and carefully deposited them on the damp ground next to the coffee cup. It seemed disrespectful somehow, to put the sugar packets—something he would likely consume—on the dirty ground, but I didn't want to approach him.

I knew I was safe. I was in full sight of everyone on Willamette Street, but I didn't know if my approach would be welcome. With no privacy, constant elemental barrage, and a whole slew of unmet basic human needs, invisible boundaries were often crossed, and I didn't want him to feel discomfort on my account.

"Time to move on," I said again. "I hope you have a good day."

I went inside the bookstore and locked the door. I'm all for basic human needs and dignity, and I know the bathroom is my first stop upon waking, but I was alone and I always keep the door locked until another coworker arrived.

I smiled to myself and turned on the store music. I did a scary thing, but it was a good thing. A human rights thing. I extended courtesy and dignity (not to mention a small breakfast) to someone in need, down on his luck, and only trying to sleep.

Buoyed by hope and pride, I finished opening the bookstore.

Later, sharing my story to my friend Scott, my mood swiftly tanked.

"You brought him food?! Great." He stomped around, throwing his arms in the air. "Now he'll go back looking for you, hoping for more. . . And he'll probably bring his friends."

My breath hitched and my heart thumped. I turned to face him, my movements stunned to slowness. I did a good thing. A *kind* thing. Tears welled and my face grew hot. Sweat prickled under my arms and along my hair. I gulped and bit down on the sides of my tongue. I didn't want to cry in front of him.

People often misjudged my tears, thinking my feelings were hurt. Sometimes they were. But that day, I was *mad.*

"I did the right thing," I gasped, still stunned by his rant. "I was *kind.*" I stood my ground even while my voice warbled.

He glanced at me, and then I felt his fear, under the anger. He'd thought I'd put myself in danger. His words were coming from a place of love, even though he was showing it poorly.

So, I turned away. Let him cool off. I surprised him was all.

I cried off and on for the rest of the day. Being the brunt of outbursts—even ones with a base of love—never felt good. But mostly, I was still angry. Angry that someone had tried to take away my power. To tell me I'd made the wrong choice. To make me feel bad for being human and being kind.

I *knew* I did the right thing that morning. And I'd do it again.

Even if sometimes I must look away when it's too much, even when I start to gulp for air and know the trigger to despair is fast approaching, *I do what I can, when I can.*

And, if nothing else, I try for eye contact.

THAT ZEBRA LOOK

Brian Cutean

Anabelle had that zebra look again; the one the nuns at St. Formica's always took the wrong way and BOOM! there goes: "Anabelle go sit in the sanctuary and say seventy-five rosaries!" and she always said 'em all somehow and now after so many unintentioned zebra looks and rosaries, she saw how it was actually better to sit alone in the quiet sanctuary for hours uninterrupted and sucked like a whirlpool in—better than having dead people snore even.

Anyoe, Mikey Spuvada put his feet in the compartment under Anabelle's seatdesk, one on either side, which usually she liked but today everything was in another language and everybody was like windup and even Mr. Galiene the custodian (who was usually the BEST person in the whole school to talk to) looked like a drawing of himself somebody on acid made. To top it off, in the middle of the night last night, Mr. Scrugglenuggles, her Persian catpet, threw up big juicy hairballs all over Anabelle's beloved 8X10 glossy picture of Solidago Walnut Hornbeam she had sent away for but it took SIX WEEKS to get it and she JUST GOT IT DAY BEFORE YESTER-DAY!!!

All of this contributed to the zebra look on Anabelle's face, which was now in progress and which Sister Perestroika hadn't noticed as of yet, just wait. Sister P. had the oddest habits of any of the other sisters there at Pius Umbeeda's Drive-Through Church and Cata-clysm Class and she was definitely not a zebra fan. Suddenly, time moved like a peach somebody runned over or stepped on and sure enough, it was yet another "Anabelle, go sit in the sanctuary and this time say eighty-three Hail Marys and sixty-eight rosaries of beer on the wall, 68 rosaries of beer . . ."

It was so quiet in the sanctuary, Anabelle could hear the drips of blood from the lifelike full-scale model of the founder and saviour hanging right there in an altared state on his own doublecross at the front of the sanctuary. After about forty-two Hail Marys, Anabelle could see the stained glass changing colour like a slow kaleidoscope. There was so much space between her heartbeats, she could slide right through between 'em and fly around for hours before the next heartbeat would come. The electrical edge of her skin reached out into seven other layers.

Suddenly, sitting next to her was the most bizarre little shrunken man all dressed up in a brown wrinkled leotard with a long funny brown cap who spoke in a shivery giggly voice. Essept he whisper without movee he lisp. "By now you recognize everything, don't you?" and Anabelle never uttered a sound when she answered, "It is always new and yet I have always known it." The brown man said, "In stillness you move through the plasma, and hypnosyncratic synaptics open and close like little fish mouths strong enough to make fish-hickeys." With that, he became a newborn baby who grew through his whole life on fast forward time lapse-leap right there in front of Anabelle. When he was the oldest man on the edge of dust, he waved goodbye slowly and made a silly face and his cells moved apart just enough for the cohesion of his aggregate form to break down, apart and through. All that remained was a faint dusting of bluish brown powder.

Anabelle smiled quietly to herself and even the drippy lifelike full-scale model up front giggled a little . . .

CRAZY PEOPLE

crazy people are an important boon
the ones who stick out and don't fit in
all talk loud and fast and then no talk for five or six months or
    years even
those ones who exude an equilibrium
of waves
emotional and musical —
emosical

crazy people pick up cool stuff off the ground
and hear every tinyest sound and yes/no
those ones eat little piles of magic irradiant food
to make their footprints twingle luminescent

you couldn't find a crazy person in a peanut shell
——————— tooooooo obvious
but crazy people put the b in subtle
and the oh! in OVERT and
they're the ones who pick up every station
on every frequent-see
in infinitesimal molecularism
so they dancing thang is brighter than arbutus
and they tuning fork careens nowheres near 440
equal tempered and carbolongonated

in perfect wisdom and effluvia,
crazy people walk like a whisper
sparkle like cardboard

dream like light blossoms
listen like smoke
chamele like rivertalk

everytime there is spiral nebulae reaching outward
everytime there is an unexpected uneasy edge
everytime there are frogs jumping out of everybunnies' pocketses
you can just sell your left toe to Hollywood
if there wasn't a crazy person plying their trade
too cool to be made
goosing elephants in the rear of the parade

Bronwynn Dean

HYDRO SOLILOQUY

The spit of mussels hissing and popping fills caves only accessible a few times a year at the lowest tides.
Echoes crashing in isolated chambers. Water drips from inside. Air is vapor. Fog so dense, you can only walk guided by the sound of the ocean.
Kelp swirls at your feet. Smells of life and decay intertwined.
Tastes of salt and infinity.
Breathing in a place that was hours ago covered by water and will soon be underwater again brings an always sense of danger, an eerie sense that you are actually underwater.
Razor clams dig holes dotting the breakline, their tracks abandoned mines.
Gulls scavenge exposed crabs, mercilessly pecking at sand dollars stranded, waiting for the water to rise.
Bodies turned inside out. A silver fish gasping for breath.
Mirages of light, rippled sand like the peaks on a stiff meringue.
Swirling volcanic black sand on every ridge, you can see the rhythm of the ocean in the print it leaves behind.
Glowing light above the fog like a soft hand on your head.
This is my backyard now.
Every day is a fresh start here. The perspective brings a new kind of quiet beyond the constant crashing and tumbling symphony.

People wait each day at sunset, that mecca on the horizon.
Watching the ocean like we are all expecting a message. A secret religion of shared experience, we smile at one another. Yes, we

witnessed this moment outside of time where the silver pathway leads to divinity. The roads full of pilgrims come to touch the sky, to the end of the earth where memory shifts with each tide. Civilizations come and gone and the ocean has greeted them all.

When you live here you become part of the storm. You are not apart from the weather. Water comes from all sides and there is nothing to do but befriend it, to become it.
The salt hag knows the tidal rhythms, the harsh pull of the moon. I measure time by tide charts and lunar phases. She knows the shore as a book of wave-tossed omens. I pick up driftwood, conjure the form hiding in its curve. I hunt for agates and measure their worth against the light.

I read somewhere the sea speaks more honestly to those willing to drown. Here, I can listen for the incoming tide without fear.

FLOCK OF BIRDS

Mose Tuzik Mosley

Ken Babbs told us that on the day Kesey died, a flock of Canada geese had taken to roost in a field across the road from Kesey's farm. It was a grey-green November day and they were driving home from the hospital, cruising down the road past Buford Park, rolling down Ridgeway Road . . . They had the top down on Kesey's white Cadillac and Zane was driving. Babbs, sprawled in the back seat, his arms spread and his big feet stretched out into the corners, had on dark glasses and was looking up into the infinite sky. As they approached the farm the birds all took off at once.

Babbs said it was a sign.

It was Kesey's spirit taking flight.

"The reason I knew this," Babbs said, "is that when all those big, mother-honking geese got halfway up into the air . . . Well . . . They took a minute to sort things out, sort out their formation, and then they made a pass over the farm. They made a big circle and then once around and I saw them from the driveway. They were flying in a big letter *K*. A perfect K-formation and they kept it up, all them white Canada geese, with the grey sky behind them, they kept it up all the way over to Mt. Pisgah."

You would have to know Babbs before you could decide if that was a true story or not, but when he told it to us we mostly believed it because that was what we wanted to believe. It was, after all, a memorial service. Memorial services are filled with suspended disbelief. It's the best time to clean up everyone's memory. Send off the deceased with some good positive vibes. Just in case they come back to haunt you later.

While Babbs was speaking, I was sitting in the balcony, up in the dark. After his story about the birds I didn't hear much more of what he said because I was suddenly thinking about white pelicans and roseate spoonbills.

I was thinking about a photo I have. It is a photo we took of my mom the last time we took her out to see the birds.

There was a wildlife sanctuary with a tower built of logs and it sat next to the estuary on the bayside of Sanibel Island. This is down toward the tip of Florida on the west side, right along the Gulf of Mexico. We took my mom out there to see the flamingos.

It was a long time ago, shortly before she died, and that year there weren't any flamingos. Just a flock of roseate spoonbills, some brown pelicans, and plenty of snowy egrets. A fine set of stand-ins, as far as she was concerned. She wasn't being particular.

It was late November, just after Thanksgiving, and she doesn't look good in the photo. Maybe it is the angle of the light, the sun going down in the middle of late-autumn clouds, the mangrove spit soaking up the image of its own reflection in the glassy waters of high tide. The birds made her smile, but the cancer had her pretty good, and her face is crooked, twisted with the effort to maintain her vision of life while she looked into the setting sun and the birds all gathered in the big old Australian pines. All gathered for the coming of night.

She died in February. On that day I was out in my father's boat, a beat-up old Boston Whaler. I was alone cruising up the Inter-coastal to the pass at Boca Grande, then putting in at Upper Captiva to swim and have a picnic lunch. Then I idled my way south along the shore, but on the outside of the islands. Smooth water, a gentle swell. I was taking my time. It was almost evening when I finally came along Point Isabella. I turned the boat northwest and the sun-set was spectacular. Just past the lighthouse at the mouth of San Carlos Bay I ran into a flock of white pelicans.

Twelve of them flying in formation two feet above the surface of the bay. The ocean was very calm, glassy, and I edged the boat right into the open part of their *V*. We flew together all the way over to the causeway. Their *V* became a big letter *R* as they flew under the drawbridge. That's what I saw. Then I eased off on the engine and watched them cruise west. They flew into a sky of rose highlights, a deepening twilight and the comforting cloak of the Florida night. I thought of my mom, Rose Tuzik. She would love to see the birds flying like that.

My Dad met me at the boat dock. It wasn't until we had the Whaler unloaded and were washing it down that he told me my mom had passed away that very afternoon. She died while I was out on the ocean. Just before I was cruising with those birds.

So now it was many years later. Seventeen to be exact. I sat in the dark at Kesey's funeral and while I sat there, I suddenly remembered that I had never told my father about those birds. Those pelicans flying in formation. Right on the day my mom died. The very day.

It took Babbs and his story to remind me, but then it was all I could think about.

At the time of that memorial service my dad was in his nineties. He was living with his third wife on Sanibel Island in that same white, wind-beaten clapboard house that he and my mom bought in the 1970s. A leaky old wood-framed Florida house perched on stilts on the canal side of Venus Drive, out near Woodring's Point.

They bought that house back in 1974 because my dad wanted a boat.

The house fronted on the water. If you could call it that. It was more of a weed infested trench that they called a "canal." Dug out of the sand and dead coral, part of it was lined with a concrete sea wall. It ran a few hundred yards into the subdivision and then branched out into shallow channels that served the various houses. This was so you could float a boat, at least a small one, in your backyard. It made the houses more expensive. "Waterfront" is what the realtors called it. Everyone wanted waterfront, including my dad.

Then, of course, "waterfront" made everything more expensive. So the house they bought, ramshackle with lots of "deferred mainte-nance," wasn't necessarily worth what they paid for it. It took all of their working-class savings plus a cash-in on their small farm in Connecticut to buy that house. It turned out to be a great investment but at the time there wasn't much left over to buy my dad a boat.

On the other hand, there were always plenty of boats for sale in South Florida. Back then it was the land of old people. Old men who were getting too old to be messing around with boats. My dad, who was still young enough to think himself a future yachtsman, found an eighty-five-year-old guy over at Fort Myers Beach. The guy was breathing out of an oxygen tube. He sold his used Boston Whaler to my dad for $1,200.

Of all the boats, and there were many, that Whaler was always my favorite. It was scratched up and well used but still unsinkable. It came with a 55-horse Evinrude, an outboard motor that stalled a lot and sometimes started. We had a lot of adventures in that boat. Me and my dad.

I don't know why these details come to mind. I certainly don't know why they came to mind at Kesey's funeral. I guess funerals are like that. You sit there and want to think about something else. As the speakers droned on, telling us what a great guy Kesey was, I was thinking about my dad trying to start that old Evinrude.

He'd be pulling and pulling at it, trying to get it to start while the Whaler drifted in the current. He'd swear at it. Take off the cowling cover and fuss with the carburetor. Put it back together and start swearing at it again. Then keep pulling and swearing until it even-tually started. I think the Evinrude was embarrassed by my father. Or maybe it was just making fun of him.

Those were great days down in Southwest Florida, before eve-rything got to be so upscale. The muddy Caloosahatchee River emptied into the Gulf of Mexico at Fort Myers, and it mixed with the ocean right there on the inside of Sanibel and Captiva. Those are barrier islands, part of a chain that stretches up toward Sarasota. A long line of islands with sandy, shell-filled beaches on the ocean side and muddle mangrove shallows on the bay side. It was my playground for a lot of those years. Mucking around in my dad's Whaler, running it aground on the low tide, sloshing in through the shallows to the beach, careful not to step on a stingray, setting up camp on Upper Captiva where there were never any people. I'd have that whole island to myself. It was paradise.

But then my mom got sick with cancer and she went very quickly, only sixty-three when she died, and somehow that ended all my innocence. I thought the universe sucked after that. I thought it was so unfair. My mom was a spectacular person. The universe just crumpled her up and took her away.

Thinking about that made me want to cry as I sat there at Kesey's funeral. It happened all those years ago and still it made me so sad. And then there was the thing with the birds.

I should have told my dad about the birds. That flock of white pelicans disappearing in the evening sky. Back then he would have understood.

It would have made sense. Now it was just a relic of the past.

Like so much else.

In all honesty I never knew Kesey very well.

And maybe you don't know him either. Ken Elton Kesey, the novel writer, original Merry Prankster, the wiz that guided us from the Beatnik Age to the Hippie Age. He was a West Coast thing. Mostly known in San Francisco and Oregon. He was by far the most famous guy in our town. I'd spent time with him but it was always with a group of people. He was always the chief, the center of attention, the head sorcerer. We were his adoring disciples. At least most of us.

My interactions with him were always one-sided. Him talking, me listening. It was hard to get a word in. But that was mostly because I didn't have much to say. Not anything of significance, anyhow.

As a person, Kesey seemed very self-absorbed, distracted by his own notoriety. I think this was a form of self-protection. He was probably trying to shield himself from idiots like me. With his kind of fame, he had a big target on his back. There was always someone out there who was willing to try to shoot him down. That sort of thing has got to fuck with you.

Still, he seemed more interested in listening to himself than to anyone else. Maybe this was his way of reassuring himself of his own importance. His own relevance. I guess this is what happens when you get famous. You find yourself trying to live up to your legend.

I'm sure I am in the vast minority here, but I don't think that people actually talked to Kesey all that much. Especially in the later years. He tended to act like some wizard with ideas about every-thing. If you listened to him, he was sure to reveal things to you. But you had to listen, not talk. And if you did talk and if you did have a good idea . . . Poof . . . He'd absorb it and make it his own and then you were listening again, now to your own idea being filtered through the great wizard mind. If you let yourself be absorbed, it could be an amazing thing to watch.

The last time I did talk to him, our last little conversation, he was about to go on stage.

It is a dark Saturday night in July. There are several thousand hippies sitting in the woods in front of the main stage at the Oregon Country Fair. I am in charge of putting on this thing we call "The Midnight Show." Kesey is going to do a five-minute cameo appearance with his grandson in tow.

We have a short conversation before he goes on. I won't re-member what we talked about. Just that I tell him I will give him a five-minute warning before it's time for him to go on stage.

He is going to make a rabbit disappear from a magic box, and show his grandson how to do it, right there in front of everyone. A perfectly orchestrated moment of grace. The wizard at the apex of his abilities. He seems a little nervous. And when he steps out into the lights there is applause, a feeling of excitement and anticipation. A big beautiful multicolored emotional wave comes up from the audience and wafts toward the stage. People are primed to love him, Kesey being Kesey.

He leans into the microphone with a bemused look.

"I said I wasn't going to say anything tonight . . . So I won't . . . Ah . . ."—pause, laughter from the crowd—"but I can't help but remember certain things . . ."

Stage lights, bright in the forest night, shine in his eyes. His grandson stands next to him, patient, holding a cardboard box with a bunny inside. A chill in the night, hardly a breath of breeze, Kesey wearing a white jumpsuit splattered with Day-Glo paint and a fifteen-gallon white cowboy hat.

"One of those first fairs, they called it something different back then, I remember the Free Souls motorcycle gang was doing the security. They had these big innertubes wrapped around their waist."

Kesey is smiling, looking into the distance.

"They wandered through the forest," he says. "These big guys, with all the tattoos and beards and long greasy hair. They had hoses that were connected to the innertubes. It turned out the innertubes were filled with nitrous. They'd take a suck on the hose and get high. They wandered the fair, and when they fell down they'd go *BOINK* and bounce back up, *BOINK* and spring up. They did a pretty good job of security . . ."

Laughter rolls through the audience. Kesey blinks his eyes. It all happens too fast. The past moving too quickly into the future. He wants it to slow down. A second more and he finds himself talking again, rambling. After a few sentences he stops himself.

"I have just one bit of magic for you tonight. We are not going to say a word . . ."

At center stage there is a stool. Kesey places a wooden box on it, its sides painted blue and red, with mystical characters inscribed in gold lettering. His hands are shaking slightly as he unclips the latch and opens the lid of the box.

He motions his grandson over. He carefully unfolds the flaps of the cardboard box, reaches in and gently cradles a white rabbit in his hands. He holds it up to show everyone.

From the audience someone shouts: "We love you, Ken!"

With a slight smile on his face he takes the white rabbit and puts it in the wooden box. He uses two fingers to push the rabbit's ears down and then with his other hand closes the lid and latches it.

No words. He steps over to his grandson and, with his hands on the child's shoulders, he moves the boy to stand directly behind the stool. Then, carefully, he begins to disassemble the box. He hands the pieces to his grandson. First the top and then the sides. The boy holds them against his chest. In a moment there is nothing left but the bottom of the box. He grasps it in his left hand and tosses it up into the night air and catches it with his other hand.

There is laughter and applause. Kesey whispers something to his grandson. They both take a slight bow. As they walk off stage, Kesey touches his hat to the audience. A cowboy farewell.

From out in the audience someone shouts: "Bring back the BUNNY!" Pause. "Is the bunny okay?"

Laughter.

Backstage, Kesey walking past me says: "Now *that* is funny . . ."

It was a moment you had to love. He touched something. Something universal. Some weird transcendence. You could hear it in his voice, a raspy quietness. An earnest appeal to kindness. A joke without a punchline that still made you smile.

He actually made a great wizard. A kind and gentle one. The kindness was what set him apart. That was his greatness.

The rest was just bullshit.

So now I was sitting with 800 other people at Kesey's memorial service. It was in the old McDonald Theatre on the main street in

Eugene, Oregon. People had come from all over to be there. The theatre was crammed to capacity. Out front was the replica *Further* bus, painted in swirls of Day-Glo, ready to carry his coffin out to the farm where he would be buried next to his son. It was an event in itself. History in the making.

When my mind came back to the moment I thought that there is so much in the world that is lost through criticism. So many things unspoken and unwritten because we fear the critics. The biggest challenge to everything creative was fear.

Whatever you had to say or think about him, you could not say that Kesey lacked courage. It was easy to criticize his writing. Easy to be jealous of his early success. But you had to acknowledge that he had put himself out there. Right out in front of everyone's opinion of him. Right in the spotlight with the target on his back glowing in the stage lights. He stood up to it all and he lasted for as long as he could. You had to hand that to him. He had a good run, maybe a great one.

So you couldn't blame those of us who wanted to be his friend. Those of us who wanted his approval and whatever lift he gave us into that magic world of acknowledgement. We were always so enamored with the idea of being famous. With the *idea* of being Ken Kesey. The same way we liked the *idea* of being Ernest Hemingway. Or Jim Harrison. The *idea* of being Mark Twain or Walt Whitman, or even a tortured soul like Melville.

We liked the idea of some regular guy, some writer, a good storyteller, a guy who led a larger-than-life kind of life. Someone who did something besides teach college. Who did not live in New York City. A guy that made himself famous by the force of his intellect and personality. Sure, the guy might be a total asshole if you got to know him. But still we loved the idea of that macho American male writer with a break-the-mold lifestyle. An icon of independence and fame. It was a guy thing. We loved it and we wanted it for ourselves. If you could shoulder up to a guy like that, a guy like Kesey, maybe some of it would rub off . . . You could get some of it on your hands and then pour it back into your typewriter. That in itself was an achievement.

I don't remember how the memorial service ended. I was so caught up in my head, in my own ideas and fears. I do remember they carried Kesey out in that psychedelic coffin and put him on the back of the fake *Further* bus. I was out there in the crowd in front of the McDonald Theatre. The street was closed off, cops everywhere. The chief mourners got on the bus and drove off to bury him at the farm in Pleasant Hill. There would be a private party and internment. By invitation only.

Surprise, surprise, I was not invited. At that point I was looking for my friends. My friends were not Bob Weir and Robert Hunter and Gus Van Sant and Sterling What's-His-Name, the famous literary agent. Nor did I know any of the other Merry Pranksters attending the memorial. I wasn't friends with the family or the inner circle. I did not have an invitation. I was not on the bus. I was not *the list*.

But I had some great friends. I had Ben Bochner and Bennet Price, who had both written a novel with Kesey. I had Scott David, the genius inventor. These were my very unfamous and very good and very long time friends. I was blessed by that.

And we had our own plan.

We were going to meet up and climb Mt. Pisgah, in the late November afternoon. At the top of the mountain there was a memorial that had been built for Jed Kesey, after he died in a bus accident. That was Kesey's eldest son. The person he would be buried next to. From up on the mountain next to the memorial we could look down on Kesey's farm in the distance. We would gather up there around the small monument, and like always we would tell each other stories. Some of them would be about Kesey . . . or at least about the *idea* of him.

Sure, we were hoping his brilliant kindness was still hovering around. A little piece or two of it might fall on our shoulders. Some wizard dust we could magically call upon.

When I was standing outside the theatre searching through the hippie masses for my friends, I did not know what was going to happen.

I did not know that we would make a collective decision to hike down the backside of the mountain. We would walk all the way down and then along Ridgeway Road and then up the driveway to Kesey's farm. We would crash the after-party. The scene at his gravesite. We would become the uninvited.

It was never a good idea. I can see that now. All these years later.

But maybe it is the only thing that makes this story worth telling. Wizard dust. The last little bit of it. Who knew where it would fall next?

Deb Casey

AUTO-CORRECT

Slavery becomes *involuntary,*
delight reads first as *drifting,* next *digest.*
As if pleasure doesn't wait. Then *imagining* appears
as *aging, alienate* as *salivate, dear* morphs
to *dare.* Hitting a hard stop mid-step
when *"A Chair for my Mother,"* reads *"Hair for . . ."*
as if to replace a place to sit
with strands to brush or braid, as if
the sink ceaselessly clogging doesn't speak
to treatments may take a toll beyond intent
asking respect: *it's a hard time,* a grandchild grants
loaning her furry dog for comfort, keeping
an eye alert maybe for wigs—not a stool
or bench might relieve these legs
that bear less easily the weight
comes of days weeks seasons not knowing: *holding*
a state absent information. Then comes *feeling* to *fringe.*
Does becomes *dies. Margins* conveniently anticipates *marginalized.*
Then *best* to *bedtime* advises with kindness: *sweet dreams*
births *suet degrees:* pecking for insight
and fuel to take flight. *Summer*
to *Simmer* moves to the stove. But
when my friend *Sheila* appears *Chisel*
and *burn* becomes *buried,* then *spell: spill:* <u>enough</u>!
Let's let go of the *old and true*-tried tries—time
the exhale gets her full due. Shake a leg.
Dare say *No.*   Undo.

FOUR DRESSES
Your Fashion-Forward Sisters Are Raving Over

Mystic misses the mark in a spacy way
        all bases lacey, flakey, flummoxed: undone
        by over-done: twisted seams seeming
        to crawl her leg tangle her tongue
        and intentions—offering no welcome surprise.
Laundry by Design
        asks a wash—stained as it is patchy.
        Modest. Maybe an invitation
        in a pocket or up
        the buttoned sleeve—waiting to be received.
Tahiti goes skimpy with fabric
        long on leg & slant—scant
        coverage calls out *hit the road:* find me
        some *skin sin—sin*-cerely some down-south fun.
The Limited
        hangs slack from spaghetti straps:
        limp drape   raving—
        craving, slave to
        drive by   dive-in   —and kicking it live.
Cloth to flesh. Sealant? Or armor.
Protection? Is that why we dress
        with such care. Push the limits. Indulge
        in looks beyond function. Jazzed designs to reveal
        conceal—seal the *dress-up* deal: seams & fabric to guarantee
the real deal's dealt.   Whether felt. Cotton. Silk. Wool
—rayon or rubber. Ever wondering what's beneath.
Rubbing the nap. Brushing against the grain
before we dare unwrap.

John Witte

PROSE

Then the words began to swim on the page my mother
stopped reading it was too much too many characters

coming and going who were these people anyway and
how had she become entangled in their lives and why

won't Nora just tell him and did Jason need to be
so nasty oh well life goes on the telephone rings

in the foyer in the novel she found herself reading
the same page over and over the characters returned

complete strangers like her son she cannot remember
the child he was lost in the prairie grass growing

darker she was awake the book a weight in her lap
like a plate of food oh well there are worse things

to lose than stories her mind for example being
swept away from shore unable to swim her voice

too faint to be heard she closes the book
the wind rippling in waves over the field

POETRY

Not words again the hydraulic craunching and creaking
of words just this pearly light on the waves what else

can we say the dawn light gleaming on the waves not this
blunt fixation of words not sublime or unforgettable but

fleeting the light gleaming as I said the waves rolling
toward us over the ocean can we be quiet now

can we go back and start again before words the waves
lifting and breaking unspoken their glory their glory

THE FOX & THE HEDGEHOG

Excerpted from the soon-to-be-published, yet-to-be-published,
never-to-be-published novel THE HEDGEHOG'S DILEMMA . . .

S.G. Ellerhoff

Having scraped his decrepit form from the unsheltered floor of a yawning dolmen, Schidder humped Herisson Wemedge onto the cart seat, shoving him upright when he sagged. He instructed him in coarse terminology from a well-meaning place that if he couldn't sit straight, he and his spines'd have to ride in the bed with the turf. The word "bed" was nearly enough to flop him snout first into the peat, but knowing the fox also hauled night soil from time to time inspired serious focus on keeping upright on the plank.

The fox fetched the hazel switch from its hook and, opting for a walking pace alongside his donkey, got things going with a whack. The ride proceeded at an easy step but the hedgehog's uneven state magnified each dip and lurch. To save from being sick, he stared through narrow lids at the straight bristling stripe down the donkey's nape, disregarding the dappled greenery of a late afternoon in spring. When a light sprinkle crossed the road, he welcomed it, waving off the fox's offer of the hat on his head.

Their backs, he knew, were to the tower.

"You the only one in your family?"

Herisson knew what the fox was asking. "I don't know," he said. "I was orphaned."

"They didn't leave a forwardin address."

"No. You?"

"Only one in seven generations." He walked beside his ass without complaint, glancing over his shoulder with a protective aspect to

184

his brindled snout. He tipped his rain-spotted hat. "I never put much in tryin to figure out the reason fer it. Lotsa reasons're lies we tell 'cause the uncertainty's too feckin scary."

"I often wonder why life changed me into a hedgehog."

"Wondrin's good. Wondrin won't trap you like shitin on about reasons does. Reasons're fer teachers 'n' arseholes 'n' arsehole teachers. I left school at eight—well, I was *asked to leave*. Did ye ever go to school?"

"Until the quills started coming in. My guardian apprenticed me early. To spare me."

"Were ye spared?"

Herisson made a noise between yes and no.

"Pricks . . ."

The rain let up. Scarcely a lone cottage and nary a man were noticed along the dreary ride through the district's open country. As twilight hued blue, dull red spots glowed where people lived, spaced irregularly across far ridges.

Herisson had finally the courage to look back.

And saw only other hills. They were long out of range for sight of Ochón Folly. The sight he hoped to see.

Schidder slowed the beast of burden as they curled a bosk of ash and holly and came upon Jack Daw's. The stonework pub loomed dark with its moss-on-slate tiled roof and stung the nose with peat smoke seeping from its three chimneys. He parked the cart in the wet grass.

"What're you doing?" Herisson eyed the door, expecting thieves to pile out and club them.

"We're stoppin fer a drink." He roped his donkey to a fence post. "No offence, mate, but yer heartbreak story is the saddest feckin thing I've heard since me Mam died." He pulled the pub door open, welcoming a billow of azure smoke into the world, and stepped indoors.

It was a quiet evening at Jack Daw's. Subdued. Standing on the flagstone floor, Herisson took in the accumulated salmagundi of raffish trinkets, dusty junk, stolen signs, and original art nailed, perched, or hung on every bit of wall, ledge, or overhead beam. The bar was teak, an antique wraparound, stooled at tight intervals. At the closest end were two stained-glass dividers, missing a pane here and there but providing some privacy should a pair seek it at the counter. An older fellow with combed white hair and a face far too nice for this kind of place pulled a pint from one of the taps. He reached blindly for a tumbler and, grasping as he set the pint aside to settle, managed to drop it.

As it smashed out of sight, he casually shouted, "Man down!"

No one else took notice.

Somehow Schidder was already down the other end of the bar, by the fireplace, holding court with four hardened men.

"I smelt a hateful aroma t'ree pints ago," one announced, "'n' I says to yer man, 'Schidder's on his way, lads.'"

"Ah, yer very good, Colm," the fox said, smacking him in the side with the wispy tip of his brush.

"Oy! Mind yer mangy feckin tail, ya quare!"

"Lads, lads," the fox yapped, "I wanna innerduce yez to me mate Wemedge. Wemedge, get yer arse over here!"

He tremored in their direction, which they noticed. The confident two, both going grey but only one bearded, were brothers: Poopdeck and Keenan. Herisson never would have guessed them kin, their features more dissimilar than alike. Poopdeck had a tightness about him, eyes and mouth cinched; Keenan was soft-eyed and serene. Then there was Shane, a man with a great height about him. Playing darts alone, he eyed Schidder and now Herisson between throws as if they weren't worth the trouble. Colm, the erratic one, was greased in sweat and crimson with drink. His inebriated aggression posed its biggest threat to his own safety. During introductions, Schidder had to grab his shirtsleeves to save him from falling rear-first into the fireplace.

"What's yer trade?" asked Shane, squaring off with the board and pitching another dart.

"He's a paper-stainer," Schidder said, swiping the darts off the board.

"Pictures, like?" Keenan asked.

"Illumination, illustration, and calligraphics," the hedgehog explained.

They quaffed their pints and smoked their cigarillos. Herisson hid behind his overbite.

"He was mixed up with yer wan up the tower down the coast," Schidder explained, chewing a dart like a toothpick. "Feckin witch fecked him out fer that spooky twat, Glibieri del Gahlo. 'Member he came in here that one time"—he changed his accent—"*ahsking for a button'f opium and two pails of shandy to quench my thirrrsty steed.* Fecksake . . ."

"That was your man who had the trouble with the jacks," said the bartender.

"What a *prick.*" Schidder about-faced and casually underhanded the darts from the waist, one at a time, in upward arcs at the board.

Two red bullseyes and a green outer bull!

"Good show," Shane muttered, stepping to the board and taking the darts for his turn.

"Where'd you learn how to do that?" he gawped. "Underhanded even!"

"Wemedge," he said, gripping the soft front of the hedgehog's shoulder, "Hang 'round establishments like this fer the drink, 'n' sure, ya pick up a few things."

"Shithead," the old man tending bar called over. He set down two fresh pints.

"Thanks, Paul Sr." The fox handed over some coins and put one of the dark ruby pints in Herisson's paws. "Get that into ya now. The stout'll 'plenish yer iron 'n' humours, even me missus has to admit that. Sláinte!" He tipped his own pint and took a three-gulp draft that left foam along his snout.

Herisson gripped the cold glass, heavy in his shaky paws. He sniffed twice at the domed head, dipped the tip of his tongue and, thirst upstaging moderation, tossed it into his mouth. Full, creamy, the beer hit the back of his throat with the most satisfying of quenchings. He tasted earth in the roasted barley. Could feel it coating the dry furrows of his shriveled stomach, unfolding the organ, filling it smoothly. And while the stout did nothing to warm his insides, it did wake him to his immediate needs, which were met in the form of a sweet, surging second pint, also on Schidder.

Bearded Keenan took pity on his broken heart with a third pint, offering up his own mysterious poetry of insight on the subject: "There's no fish without the river."

Whatever that meant, the fox had vanished to make his rounds, seeing to others who'd not been there when they arrived.

"Why'd they call this place Jack Daw's?" Herisson asked, thinking he was asking Keenan, whom he thought was on his left.

The answer came from his right. "'Cause this was Jack's pub," said an elder toad, all speckled in freckles. "Now he's stuffed in the corner, so he is, as per his dyin wish . . ."

Herisson turned and peered into the dim corner, finding there, sure enough, the black shape of a man-sized jackdaw, clear-blue glass eyes twinkling. Having never in his life encountered anybody mummified through taxidermy, his quills shivered up and down his hunched back.

"S'what he wanted," the toad said. "S'what he got. How many in death can say as much?"

Natterjack—that's what the old toad said his name was—asked what brought him to the bar and he looked for the fox to point to him but, not finding him, again blamed heartbreak. Not missing a beat, the old-timer told Herisson all about a woman he was having an affair with in the Big Shmoke more than forty years earlier.

"In them days I was bald as I am this day and, despite bein a toad, I wore a toupee, so I did. I was romancin yer wan with this cap o' brown curls atop me head, 'n' me thinkin she didn't know they were, mmm, en*hanced*. Me missus back home, she knew! I knew well enough she knew, so I did, for all the attention she gave me for bein a hairless toad. But there I was, in another city with another woman an' we strollin along the quays one morn after workin all night. We shtopped, I remember like we're still there, on Belfry Bridge, overlookin the river, an' she askin, 'Natterjack,' she asks, 'why d'ya wear that thing?' An' she took it right off an' chucked it into the drink, where it sunk like a stunned rat." His great gold eyes brimmed wet. "Ara, how I loved my Ann, more'n I ever could love me own Maureen. An' both of 'em *dead* now!" The poor old toad fell to weeping on his stool.

"Ah grand, the auld frog's so pissed he's cryin," Schidder, suddenly at his side, said out the side of his mouth.

Natterjack's pebbly face glistened with tracks streaming from his bulging eyes. "I wouldn't be fond o' cryin' but I means it, every tear! So I does, so I does . . ."

By now it was unclear how many pints Herisson had indulged—likely just the three he could recall—and while he felt sorry for this new friend's grief, he was all too aware of his own and relieved by Schidder's return. Things had picked up since arriving, a few more patrons wandering around, including a quite tall server lady dressed in plain linens without, he couldn't help noticing, a corset beneath.

"Takin a shine to Dymphna, are ya? Already onto the next woman—that's it!"

"No, no."

"Dymphna!" he yapped. She came right over with a tray of empty glasses. Herisson shrank, his orbicularis muscle twitching.

"Aye, wee Schidder!" She wrapped her free arm down around the fox and he rubbed his dark tufted cheek into her bosoms with shut eyes and lolling tongue, the expression exaggerated for Herisson's benefit. She spread her upper lip in a grin that lined parallel to her fringe, cut straight just over her eyes. "Ya come back for me to change yer nappy, did ya?"

"Ooh, change my nappy, change my nappy," Schidder pleaded, chin to breasts with eyes looking up at her. "I only done a piss fer ya this time!"

The two of them heaved laughing, leaving Herisson to wonder. Natterjack sniffled.

"Wemedge, this's Dymphna, me auld wet nurse from when I was just a teat-suckin kit."

"Ya lyin fox!" she brayed. "Ye never had a suck off these!"

"Maybe not, but I can't tell ya how many times I've brung meself off thinkin about it."

"Dirty, dirty fecker!" She grabbed his scruff and gave him two hard shakes. "I used to look after him," she explained, "when his parents needed *a break*. Ye can imagine, I'm sure…"

Making acquaintances, she, too, asked what he'd like to drink. Picking up on the fact that he hadn't eaten, Schidder ordered him a ham-and-cheese toastie and a side of dried prawns. He ordered the same for himself, promising they could get an order of boxties on their way out if they were still hungry.

A pat on the belly and the fox was gone again. Dymphna was gone, taking care of the order. Even Natterjack had left the next stool. Having a look around, there the old boy was, turning a spry slip-jig on the flagstones. The trousered toad cut a spirited figure, smacking his hands for the odd downbeat clap to the trad session

Herisson had missed starting. There was a fellow on guitar without any hair up top and a white mustache of impressive dimensions, a ginger fiddler with all the embellishments of a player who'd spent a night's month with the Good People, and a girl, no older than ten with black plaits pinned in a crown, tooting a tin whistle just as natural as breathing. They were well into it, not at all dependent on anyone taking notice.

He sat and swayed, not with rhythm but with sorrow. The tune, sprightly, provided no protection. His shame—for being so very wrong about how the Solar Witch felt about him—left him stumped. Stupid.

The hedgehog was verging when Dymphna returned with a pint of ale, a steaming ham-and-cheese toastie, and pile of crunchy prawns on the side. She asked what was wrong, listened as she tended to the particulars of making sure his sandwich got a slathering of mustard. A nurse in barmaid's dress. Her pity at his haltingly narrated heartbreak both professional and kind. She even knew when and how to flirt with him.

"Aren't you just the sweetest thing?" She set one half of his toastie perpendicular atop the other. "I'd just *love* to corrupt you!"

"Well," he said.

Dymphna scratched his furry cheek. "Now you just get stuck into that toastie now, ya starved darlin. You don't wanna be emancipated!"

He knew what she meant.

She was gone again but the sandwich was present. The salted ham and melted cheese tasted as good in his mouth as they smelled in his nose. Hunger, in this moment anyway, disregarded the pain, superseded its authority over him. And when Schidder reappeared, he asked him why, if this was such a dangerous place, there happened to be a little girl there playing tin whistle?

The fox used Herisson's napkin to brush the crumbs out of his fur. "Murd'rers 'n' thieves 'n' gurriers 'n' messers 'n' brigands have kids, too, mate."

Herisson pondered the musical girl, wondering which one of the treacherous men in the pub was her father.

Both of them still hungry when came time to push home, Schidder ordered boxties for the road and went around saying goodbye in various inappropriate ways. Here, it seemed, no one cared what anybody happened to be. Jack Daw's seemed a haven for anyone who wandered in, no matter his station or circumstance, so long as it was one familiar with struggle.

When their potato pancakes came up and Dymphna splashed them with vinegar and hailed them with salt, and it was time to head, Herisson, who'd paid for nothing, expressed the thanks he could with speechless nods and a smile that must've looked to others like torment. The hardened bad men—Keenan and Poopdeck and Shane and Colm—were all as casual to his leaving as they'd been to his coming.

Schidder reached past him and pushed the door open, cold air slugging him at once, and out they went. While the fox untied the donkey, the hedgehog's duty was to not drop the parcel of boxties.

"Those guys were great," he said.

"Those guys're 'sponsible fer a buncha killins up the Gully Gap that ever'body knows they done but can't pin on 'em."

"Really?"

Schidder placed his paws on Herisson's shoulders and gave him a fierce intelligent look with his yellow-green, night-bright eyes. "Mate, only reason ya got in there without harm comin to ya is 'cause I was there. 'N' now they know yer with *me*, ye'll never have to worry 'bout anybody doin anythin to ya. They know yer sound."

This fox was the sort of friend someone hoping to stick around should like to have on his side. He didn't particularly feel like sticking around, but if he did . . .

Herisson made it into the back of the cart with a heave and a push and soon they were off through a lazy rain toward Schidder's home. The donkey knew the road and took it at pace, ignoring the pair of drunks.

"Why'd she get rid of me?" he groaned, heaped upon the turf briquettes.

"'Cause she's an arsehole," Schidder barked from the plank.

"How do you know that?" He asked this knowing that he himself was sauced but not so sauced that the question didn't register as a foolish one to ask out loud.

"I know lotsa things, ya big prickly gobshite—one of 'em bein ya shouldn't ever go back to Ochón Folly. *That*," he reiterated, "I know."

He explained on the way that his missus, Marisol, had a Tarot Master Class that night, so she may or may not be home when they got there. He'd have to clear it with her, Herisson being allowed to stay, but he didn't anticipate it being a problem after she saw the state of him. Wagner, the dog, definitely would be home, and hopefully he'd have the fire going, though, being a regular dog, they oughtn't get their hopes up.

The countryside this night was wet, windless. The two, pulled by the third, were intoxicated, though one could hold it far better than the other. Sprawled stomach-down with not the strength to close into a ball, Herisson felt in need of looking after.

It turned out to be a proper house, Schidder's home, grown over to elegant effect in ivy. A hazel tree, growing catkins of pale tinsel, stood out front. Schidder brought the donkey around the hedge, drawing the cart under the tree. Its decorated branches reached overhead and, sitting up and taking a sniff of the dangling aments, Herisson sneezed. Spring, with its resurgence, brought allergies.

Schidder, releasing the donkey from its yoke, slurred through an explanation of how his mammy, when he was a baby, took the still-green nuts from that tree and prepared from their milky centers a mush, laced with honey. It was his first solid food, provided by this selfsame tree in the yard.

"Before your change?"

"That's right, before. When I was still a baby boy."

Herisson spanked the peat dust out of his trousers and trailed after his host, past potted plants placed in no specific arrangement along the walk. The windows were not lit. Schidder, swaying before his door, crouched and tilted one of the large pots holding a wilted flop of primrose leaves. He scuffed his toes under the lip, scooting out a fat black key.

A dog on the other side of the door started barking.

"It's just me, yer poor decrepit alcoholic father!" Schidder was jabbing the key everywhere but the keyhole. The dog inside kept barking.

"Wagner! You pipe down right this instant! Bad Wagner!"

He got the door open and out scuttled a little white dog with short legs and a stubby tail going back and forth. Into Schidder's arms it leaped and they both of them licked the other's nose and whined back and forth.

He introduced the cradled Wagner to Herisson, dog and hedgehog both flattening their ears.

"Say hello to yer Uncle Wemedge, Wagner! Say hello to yer Uncle Wemedge!"

Hellos were exchanged and Schidder conducted them into the house, inviting Herisson in as he repeated everything he'd said about him being welcome—though he'd need to check with the missus—who was likely still out—but he should make himself at home all the same. The house was bigger than he assumed it would be, and when the fox managed to light a lamp it revealed a room alive with nearly as many plants indoors as those growing up its outer walls. Cases brimmed with books and framed pagan symbols. The furniture was leather-cushioned with spare blankets, folded and waiting to be unfolded, within arm's reach no matter where one sat.

The fox shoved a boxty into his mouth and chewed with loud smacks. "Jeekers, I'm *starvin*!"

They took to mismatched footstools by the hearth, and the fox set a fire. When the turf lit, Herisson let Schidder finish off the pan-fried spuds. Tossing his felt hat at the wall, the fox brought the hidden naggin from off his head for its final drop and then threw it toward the hat on the floor. When Wagner made for the door, barking with the might of a hound despite his small frame, he didn't even glance.

"That'll be Marisol. Home from Tarot Master Class."

Herisson hadn't spent a thought wondering about Schidder's vixen and realized he really didn't know what to expect. Coarse? Likely. Dowdy? Probably. But this décor, with the plants and sigils, and her taking classes from the High Priestess, these details suggested more than a harridan. And just when he got to wondering if her coat would be red or brindle or maybe even black, she called in from the doorway—"Hello there, Wagner! Is your feckless father home or do we have the place to ourselves?"—and he turned to see that, indeed, her coat was red, but made of tailored wool, not fur.

Schidder stood fast, nearly tripping, and swept his bedraggled brush across Herisson's eyes in the process. Squinting, he rose, too, the fox pulling him upward.

"Can we keep him?"

"You're joking."

Marisol, it turned out, was a woman. The very kind a hedgehog would feel too shy to speak to if encountering her under circumstances where he wasn't going to be introduced. Her long coat, holly-berry red, bore fox-faced brass buttons down its front. Her hair, braided into a messy chignon, was a rainbow of every natural tone a woman's hair color might be. Chestnut locks wove with mousey locks wove with auburn with blonde with cinnamon, all shades into sable and some grey and some white—he'd never seen a head like it. And where her eyes, shadowed with glittering turquoise, were bright and slightly perturbed, they were also bright and clever. Confidence and vulnerability, soul and a sense of humor, all present and humbling upon meeting her.

Schidder had done very well for himself. Herisson fell meek.

"Marisol, d'yez 'member that fella I got on with up the Solar Witch's place?"

She sized Herisson up warily, hanging her bag over the back of a chair. "I do."

"Right, well. This's him: Me auld flower, Herisson Wemedge!"

"Of course!" She addressed him directly now, taking interest and holding one hand up to her husband's muzzle. "Can I get you a drink? Did he offer you one?"

"Well, he—"

"Aucnus Schidder, you're a shithead." She walked out of the room, emerging from her red coat on the way. "Bringing a guest into our home and not offering him a drink…"

Schidder nudged him. "Yer in."

She returned with a mug of cider for Herisson and instructions that her husband could get his own if he was thirsty, which he oughtn't be, seeing as he must've already been drinking plenty to be as pissed as he happened to be. He pretended to sleep on one of the couches while she settled into a balding-velvet wing chair to make nice with the visitor she never knew was coming. Herisson, to his credit, was polite enough to take the stool again, knowing his spines would scratch any seat with a back. He sipped the cider. It puckered the gums to his teeth.

"So you met Aucnus at the tower then." The dog hopped into her lap to curl there like a cat.

"That's right, that's right." Herisson cupped the drink in his hands, feeling shy. And so very tired.

"He never told me you were a hedgehog."

And so, for the third time that same day, the ordeal of Herisson's present condition found itself narrated to someone else. Where the fox earlier took vulgar liberties at Jack Daw's, he now abridged the tragedy, only with the addition of occasional backtrackings. By story's end, all were caught up on the sorry present of one broken-hearted Herisson Wemedge. And all were also more than ready for bed.

"I'll just crash here 'n' piss the sofa," Schidder said to his missus, "so ye'll not have to worry 'bout me pissin the bed, Luv."

She wasn't having that, so onto their hind legs they clambered. Each receiving a peck on their furred cheeks from that most radiant lady—undoubtedly more so than Sorcha, he had to admit—the fox led the hedgehog down the hall to the guest room. Schidder went around the room pointing out things like candleholders, vases, creaky floorboards and before he knew it Marisol passed in a cup of warm milk spiked with valerian root for him to drink. The concoction drank smooth and slaked his fatigue and Schidder and his paltry tail were leaving him to it before he knew it.

Bedding down belly-down, calmed with sleep close by, Herisson heard Schidder and Marisol rowing in their room on the other side of the ivied house.

"What was I s'posed to do, Marisol? He'd've perished if I'd not drug him off that hill!"

"I don't have a problem with him! He's grand!"

"But he's got nowhere to go! That twat kicked him out 'n' left him fer dead—he was hibernatin in a feckin ruin without leaves or nothin fer shelter, exposed to the elements, no scrap o' nothin to cover his bones!"

"Just don't feck things up with your wan, Schidder."

"Don't you be tellin me how to conduct myself!"

"She's your last steady contract!"

The door nosed open, claws clicking on hardwood, and something leaped onto the bed. Wagner, fleeing the fight, turned twice at Herisson's ankles and plopped down on top of the blankets.

"He feckin balls up at the whiff'f nothin!"

"And I told you he's grand, you daft eejit!"

"He's not so wily as me! He's a defensive creature!"

"Stop giving out and go the feck to sleep, you fleasome gobshite!"

"You feckin go to sleep, ya gobrot!"

His last thought before sleep was for Schidder and how he'd picked him up and pulled him out of that drafty old dolmen when others would've trundled on—and how that spoke more to the fox's character than common prejudices categorizing his pedigree. And though hurt, he felt safe in this house. He felt sure, with a just-met dog snoring at his feet, that he'd come into a fatefully fortunate friendship.

Mending seldom, if ever, culminates as a single event. Setbacks open like rifts, often enough with one foot set uncertainly on either side of the parting chasm. Too often there isn't time to hop to one side or the other, and one tumbles back into the pit.

Not long into his recovery, on a night the moon turned scarlet, Herisson fled the ivied cottage under the cover of silence, knowing his hosts would stop him. Through the stilled woods he followed that murdering moon. Adrenaline answered this dark night of the soul's dictum and on he loped, numb to the footfalls, toward the place he knew he should not return.

He encountered no one on the road, no wildlife either. Night birds held silent. Trees did not speak. All that sounded was the blood drumming in his ears. All he saw was the red disk of the moon summoning him over the damp hills, one after the other.

This clotted desperation gave way to the prodigious hill called Ochón Head. The moon, gone the color of wine on stone, coaxed him up the moss-striped lane and through the copse of naked elders. He rounded the great boulder where the tower of Ochón Folly stood in its own shadow, candles burning at the third stage. Her bed-chamber window, which he'd only ever seen battened, glowed faint with brown light.

The apple tree, in bloom, smelled like white gold, rich in the still air. He halted under its flowered boughs when catching the outline, on the other side of the clearing, of the stable. The Lunar Alchemist's pearlescent carriage stood outside, meaning his horse must be inside. He would announce his own arrival, not be given away by a skittish whinny.

If, that is, he decided to announce he'd come.

He didn't really know why he was here.

Herisson drew to the steps and found above the door, where the sun's face was carved in relief, fresh carving, a crescent lined over the circle and donating one eye to a superimposed moon. The two celestial spheres now stood out in sickled eclipse over the threshold. That was new.

And he saw how good things were meant for others—not for him—a figure of no consequence. There came a sudden cry from the wound he'd been dealt at this place. Racked, he tumbled, falling hard against the steps. He lifted his arms, wanting to ask the world around him why any of it had happened. Without answer coming, he dropped them.

Tucking limbs under, Herisson balled himself shut upon the cold stone stoop, no intention of unfurling his tender side for anybody or anything.

But he could not close his ears. However folded they happened to be, they picked up the now familiar clop of a certain gait paired with a known wheel creak. And close after, the yawping incredulity of a friend who'd gone to some trouble.

"Wemedge! Fecksake!"

There was a scuffling of paws on path, unmistakable musk.

"C'mon, mate, stop bein a bollix," the fox barked from the other side of his spines. "We gotta get yous outta here before those wankers cop on."

"*Who's down there?*"

"Ah feck!" Schidder hissed.

Herisson didn't budge. He held himself tighter with shame.

"Listen, his sword's longer'n those pricks on yer back—he'll run ya clean through."

"Let him," Herisson said to himself.

"*Who's down there at this hour?*"

"Ahhh feck," Schidder muttered, tamping his hind paws. "Can't believe I'm doin this."

The distinctively subtle sound of a fine, concentrated stream of fluid conspired with the sensation of a growing spot of steaming hot wetness on Herisson's back to inform him that the fox was, indeed, pissing on him.

Unballing, Herisson emerged, complaining, but found himself snatched up under his arms and hauled in haste to the donkey cart waiting between the apple trees.

"You *peed* on me?"

"I *pissed* on ye. Yer man'd do worse if he found ya blockin the door come mornin." He hustled back to the tower's door, as if he'd forgotten something there.

"What're you doing?"

Schidder crouched to a squat at the top of the steps, bent his wiry brush more or less straight, and dropped one—two—three oily black turds upon the stoop.

Breaking for the cart, hand on hat, the fox forsook stealth for speed and heaved himself onto the plank behind the donkey. The tower door opened and the Lunar Alchemist came forth with lit lantern and open-toe sandaled foot skidding through Schidder's feces.

"*What in—*"

"Ah yeh," Schidder yapped over his shoulder. "That'd be me letter'f assignation ya just stepped in."

Though wearing only a robe, he was armed, sword in scabbard at his waist. He lifted and stared at the sole of the soiled sandal. "*Did you—*shit *on my doorstep!*"

"Be a good lad 'n' tell the witch I've quit, del Gahlo."

"*It's gel Dahlo!*"

"Yeh, grand!" The donkey trotted without a tap from the hazel switch. "Yer wan can find another mongrel to shovel out her shite. I've had me fill."

The man with the lantern and fox poop between his toes did not fetch his horse or give chase. He stepped back into the tower, shaking his head, likely never even seeing the listless heap in the back of the cart. Would he have known who that bramble was? Would she have told him?

The dull light in her bedchamber window showed no flicker of disturbance. Herisson did not see her move in her high room. Soon the nude trunks of the elders came in the way of the tower and he knew it wouldn't feel like she was gone for some time yet. There was, in life, a division between endings and their recognition as such. It was strange knowing this without the power to transport himself to that end. A sensing of destination without map, timetable, or directions with regard to eventually arriving. He simply knew, watching the top of the tower roll away behind tree and hill, that his time at Ochón Folly was truly done.

The moon's murdering aspect had shifted, its white cheek returned. No more blood. He watched it through the woods' budless arms with his lightless black eyes.

It occurred that, though he didn't currently feel it, he ought to show some gratitude for Schidder's trouble. "Thanks for fetching me."

"Fetching you!" The fox wouldn't turn to look at him. He hunched forward. "The ass was knackered after a full day 'n' I was already in bed quarrelin with the missus when Wagner comes in lettin us know yez was gone. Scared me outta me wits, you did. 'N' now I gotta tell the missus I lost me biggest contract . . ."

He'd gone and ruined Schidder's livelihood, taken food out of his and Marisol's mouths. "I'm so sorry," he mumbled with even greater shame.

"I know ya are . . ." He leaned back and took a flashing look with his yellow-green eyes at his friend. "Sorry fer pissin on ya."

"Oh it's alright." He started to stretch to sniff and tell if he smelled like urine but stopped.

"I should'a been lettin ya air yer mind 'n' all. S'part'f the healin process, mate."

They fell quiet to the turn of the cart's two wheels and the donkey's hoof-falls. He thought about how fast she'd turned away from him, how fast she'd been to bed him to begin with, how she often watched the moon rise from the sea terrace and how he never made the connection between the moonstone pendant always worn around her neck and another man.

"If I'd just—"

"If you'd just—*if you'd just* . . . Listen t'me." Schidder reached and twisted the fur on Herisson's chest. "I can't tell what's a mad move and what isn't no more. I've seen eejits gain from their feckin eejit tactics and noble lads fail with sound hearts 'n' ways. It's a feckin waste land. 'N' here's the problem. That witch already had the big story'f her life goin on before ya showed up. Yez was just a walk-on part. Unfortunate fer ye, ya walked into a story already underway. *Chapter Fifty-Nine: The Hedgehog Arrives. Chapter Sixty: Feckface Returns 'n' Gives It to Her in the Arse Again.* She 'n' that twat had unfinished business 'n' no amount'f you doin anythin at all'd make a shite'f a diff'rence. Those two're made fer each other. When*ever* an ex shows up, if so-n-so's compelled to give 'em more'n a 'hi, hello, feck off now,' there's still love there, or somethin like it. Let 'em wank each other off in their feckin big feckin cock folly'f a tower. Yer just not a part'f her feckin story, mate, sorry. If she gave two shites about ya, ye'd still be in there gettin yer hole. That's the truth."

Herisson imagined the physical distance between him and the Solar Witch lengthening also in spirit. He had never been all that close to Sorcha. He had only wanted to be.

"I can get business back on track again with a bit'f help, score a few more contracts, bigger contracts. Two hedgerow landscapin shitemongers is better'n one. Two lads, twice the work, each job finished twice as fast. We could team up. Me 'n' you. We'll shovel shite, plant a few shrubberies, get pissed at Jack Daw's on the daily."

The hedgehog blinked his tearful eyes in the direction of clarity.

"Whaddaya say, Wemedge? Will ya gimme a hand?"

Of course, he said, "Yes. Of course."

Elly Bookman

WHITE COLLAR

Instead it's my job
to scrub the underside
of the dish sink. At

the end of a shift, tip-
laden, lonely, starched
white shirt spotted

with soup and grease,
like a mechanic I lie
on my back and scour

the metallic underbelly
where dinner morsels
and mold have amounted

to a layer of black glue,
lips pressed in a line
of defense against

whatever came loose.
Later, in my kitchen
I soak the shirt in

my own sink, hang it
to dry, then iron
anew the one I wore

the shift before. Over
the radio, a voice says
the stocks have fallen

and fallen. Tomorrow
is the drip on the
tile floor I ignore.

POEM

At last I laid my hands
on the one about

the airport and the lover.
And I know I'm not supposed

to let a poem tell me
my life, but let me explain.

It is pre-dawn dark, the moon
is still in the sky

and is my favorite kind
of crescent and I'm sipping

something hot and
eating cold wedges of fruit

and remembering the first time
I held this book, walked

home from the library
reading

which isn't something
I normally do but

that afternoon the sidewalks
were just empty enough

and I hardly
had to cross any streets

and the poem was
murky. Wide, opaque

puddle of things I'd never
quite felt. And now

that it is too late for stars and
too soon for sun

the only thing up there besides
the moon are

satellites and planes
carrying signals and lovers

and one of them
mine. Poem,

poem whose waters have rushed
over the rocks in me

all these years, could you
run clear now?

No, it turns out.
But you are as necessary

an unquenched mystery
as ever.

CODE RED

While schoolchildren slip
like stolen hours into the corners
of the room, I turn
the half-disc of the lock
from horizon to high noon
then flip the little lever
of the light switch and like this
we have followed instructions,
we have done what we can.
The weather will be
what it is—several minutes
of sunshine or clouds,
maybe the kind of mist
you only know is falling
if you see it against gray road
or thick trees—inevitable,
exact result of every
wind, pressure, and breath
of earth's whole history
here rendered.
In darkness,
I remember the day
a heavy volume of landscapes
by Hitler came into the used
bookstore where my job
was to tenderly wipe down
the covers, then wrap the jackets

in clear plastic. Inside
were Austrian countrysides
and town squares, Alpine
villas and lakes as clear as
emptiness. A man
saw the world and sought ways
to make it look more like
how it feels to be lonely.
I remember this
now, now my job is to wait
for the noises to be
what they are, for the smells
and textures, the colors
of the air, of
the walls and floors.

AN OLD-TIME LOCAL-INTEREST STORY

Scott Landfield

It was the end of the world in South Eugene. Another long day in hell. No big deal.

A number of us were seated around a small cluster of rickety but clean enough tables on a high spot of the tilted floor by the glass-free windows of what in the good old days was known as Turtles, which, by reason of the innumerable defaults of general disaster, proudly bears the name Turtles once again. The cold summer rain rumbled on the piece of roof that doesn't yet leak, that we gather under most every evening around dusk, to watch the puddles drain away, either deep into the dark old building where Old Bill, who in his youth marched for peace from North Carolina to Eugene in a pair of Birkenstocks, then presided as the best bartender in a booming town, and now is back, thankfully, through this final bust; or else to just watch it stream down the short slope to the impassable, broken concrete of Willamette.

Like everyone else every day these days, probably everywhere, we were waiting for the deeper shadows of night, the best time to scrabble off to our various warrens of comfort and hiding. All things considered, we have it pretty good on this side of College Hill, here in what we used to call beautiful South Eugene. For one, there were enough nuclear fallout shelters built into the homes just up the hill after the Second World War of the last century that there are plenty of comfortable caves to be had, places to strike out from each day to make a stab at a piece of this century for those of us left. And another thing—the best—we were all drinking liquor, waiting on the meat, taking turns telling stories, celebrating the simple glory of another day.

"How does Old Kate do it? How does she keep this place in liquor," wondered Old Sky, whom everyone thought had died in the boom years, but as it turned out had just been the first one to retire from sight. That Sky, he's the only one can get away with calling Kate "Old" Kate without either hurting her feelings or pissing her off. Sky, with that giant green stuffed-toy puffin he always brings with him to the bar. Kate, who for a memorable few years ran the best restaurant and bar in America, every clean new table surrounded by happy people around huge platters of good food and freely poured drinks, the bar a long piece of rare koa wood filled with as rare a crowd of well-polished characters, a room full of people always celebrating something back in the day.

Damn.

Old Rob leaned in, cleared his throat to speak. Everyone leans in when Rob leans in, preparing to stretch a tale. Again, a guy rumored to be dead. But there are many of us who should be dead. It's always a wonder who lives and who dies. Rob, a scion from Connecticut, a genius, great musician, and imbiber of mass quantities of whatever; at one time an especially handsome blonde, short and wired, who used to supplement his various modest trusts with occasional work in whichever was the most exciting, popular, heroic kitchen in Eugene at that brief moment; and had more than once been classy kitchen help for Kate, and still had the skinny.

Old Rob, he's the one who famously figured out these troubles we're in first began with the leash laws for dogs in the late sixties—the funniest, saddest, truest story you've ever heard.

"Kate told me she got this particular batch of booze from that raunchy tribe lives under the old cherry tree near the river in the Whit. Took them three days to get up here. You can taste the fresh runoff, with just a hint of berry scat from the old park across from the old DeFazio bike bridge. When it fell in the river it changed the current. Makes for the best blend."

Old. It's a word we use too much these days. But everything that's left is old; that, or broken. Plus, old is the link to when we ruled the world—the world—sometimes with an innocent, sometimes an arrogant disregard. Old, simply, is all we've got, unless you include each new day. And even if it were possible, which it isn't, it would take a lot of brand spanking new days to get this mess back to the way it was, least so far as choice and comfort and disregard. And by then we'd be really old, that or dead. As is, this getting old thing is way overrated.

I say leave the getting old to the young. Although I really don't want to leave them anything. I mean, I'd like to leave them something, like maybe a whole new world. But think about it: considering who it is who taught them what they know, who knows how they'd fuck it up?

These poor young folk, the few left, have it hard these days, not being old, having to figure out how to survive, wondering why they even should. Seems death by suicide is the norm now, young people ending it, even ritually so.

One thing I'd like to tell these kids, though, is if you're going to end it, stay calm. Remember, it's the adrenalin of a horrific death that spoils the meat, turns us mean when it goes sour in our bellies. Just think about those hordes on the other side of the river, how crazed they were from the barbecue they had of those bodies festering in the Stadium after the last sanctioned rage.

"A toast to Kate, and to the return of our favorite barkeep, Old Bill, who measures his pour to a drinker's need, and still tells the best jokes in town," intoned Old Dennis, a tank commander in one of the many wrong wars, who later made his living maintaining the 11,427 doors of the former University on the far east end of town. He's the man who saved old Civic Stadium from greedy corporate hands, only to watch it burn down in a hot hour, torched by a kid who people said set his own grandma's house on fire the previous day, this long before the real trouble began. Old Dennis, his still-red beard hanging low, braided, which he uses as suspenders to help keep his pants up when sneaking back to that flower-strewn shack where he holes-up with his beautiful wife, La Reina.

"That's because there's always such fresh material," quipped Old Bill, eyes aglow from behind the little piece of koa wood bar that remained. Somehow, just the way he said it caused us to erupt in a phlegmy, necessary group laugh, a moment we live for, as long as we each may live.

"Hey Bill," called Old Shankar in his friendly, high-pitched undertone. Shankar, a former marine turned banker, who can still mesmerize with tales of the old days of rock and roll; the only born-and-raised local boy among us, though clearly his mother, whom he lovingly tends, came from halfway around the world, back when we thought of it as a world. "Bill, this high-octane blackberry mash is more than we dare expect under the present audacities, but what's taking so long with the meat?"

"The meat's on its way, gentlemen," chimed Kate, coming out of the deep shadows. "The crew is just now putting the final singe to it in the alley. Took a little longer than usual finding the wood for the fire. But it's the best left in the neighborhood, an untreated, still dry twelve-by-four old growth floor joist from what's left of that house up Twenty-Second we've been pirating away. Apparently the crew got into a little tussle with some scavengers from down in the old Friendly Neighborhood who were up to the same no good as us."

Old Kate—excuse me, that is to say Kate—came from what used to be Durango. Evel Knievel's kid sister. Plus, she had ten years in the military. She started Turtles near the end of the Final Millennium, and started it right. It was a place where a woman could sit at the bar, alone, and drink, eat half a meal and take the rest home, and never be hassled, neither by man nor woman; which in fact is why most of us "gentlemen" came to be regulars, men constitutionally circumspect with women, though always enjoying their company from two stools away.

Turtles, a family-friendly roadhouse where never a fight was brewed; where the bartenders and waitresses bought nice little pads, paid for with the tips they earned; and where some lucky few are rumored to still reside.

Remember 9/11? An argument could be made that, except for the leash laws, it was the first hint of this final mess we're into; that is, if you were fool enough to look back in such sad directions. What I remember is a 3X5 notecard on the Turtles front door, back when there was a front door, with a black felt-tip note scrawled by Kate that read "*All proceeds from today's fare go to the Red Cross.*"

The place was packed, the big screens turned off. Everyone was talking at once, same as always, only in hushed tones.

"Hey Kate! You got a name for tonight's meat," called Old Sky, feigning innocence, leaning into his old Puffin friend, who somehow always claimed the one sturdy chair left in the joint.

Back in the day the tall menu read "*barbecued beef ribs, blackened salmon salad, garlic chicken, surf and turf, locally raised half pound hamburger, big salad.*" Now, the deer, the wild turkeys, even the frogs are gone. The bear and coyote know to stay away. The dogs and cats, well, never mind. The rats of course are everywhere, wily and dominant on this stinking ship of a planet, where it's best to simply call the day's communal platter "meat." *Meat.*

Kate, never one to take a joke without giving back double, stepped up, leaned back, and prepared to whip some snide-ass remark on Old Sky, for the entertainment of all, including Sky.

At that very moment Old Booker, soaking wet in an ancient military greatcoat, suddenly entered the bar, climbing in through the empty window frame nearest our crowd. He took his usual seat, in what would be the lookout position anywhere but Turtles, a look of more than the usual horror in the black orbs burning behind his thick grey beard.

An end-of-the-world quiet filled what was left of the room. Everyone's eyes were upon him, wide with wonder, soft with compassion. He waved to someone outside, who leaped in with a youngish step, a fellow perhaps forty, little more than a boy in today's childless world. He stood there next to Booker, nodded to each of us, a possum skin cap mashed down on his long, thick black-haired mess of a handsome head.

Young Bob, a fellow we always like to see. If there's hope in hell, that's what Bob gives us. He was hugging a ragged bag rough-stitched from an ancient hickory shirt. It was sopping wet and, in the deepening dusk, appeared to be stained red.

Old Booker. He owned the Bookstore, about a block down from Turtles, on what used to be the main street, Willamette, like the mighty river, where it used to begin. They called it Tsunami Books, had a mural of Hokusai's Great Wave across the top, with fanciful natural images of books melded with nature below, including a trio of Northern Spotted Owls in an old growth forest reading a copy of *Cronies*, and what looked to be a 400-pound neighborhood homeless kitty cat named Swirly, hauling a cart of books and the usual banana slugs and snails in the direction of the garden entrance.

Funny thing, poor bookseller that he was, once these end-times first came to a false crest, he finally started making a whooping good living, riding the wave of people's now insatiable need for books, preferably long ones, to read in asylum, waiting for whatever the fuck was happening to be over. Far as any of us know it was the only undamaged building in town, right up until, yep, you guessed it, someone burned it down five days ago, no doubt torching it with the flick of an ancient, precious Bic.

Damnit! So the lowest dirty bastards didn't all die.

They never do.

Kate broke the silence.

"I'm so sorry, Booker dear, that Bookstore meant the world to the whole neighborhood. Where you been, honey? Bill, bring him a drink. And one for the boy."

Old Booker clutched his beard with both gnarled hands, pulled down, his lips pried open, displaying six bright false uppers and two black nubs below in a full grimace. He took a deep breath, sobbed once, then began in a calm, quiet, faraway voice.

"The books were all I had. The only thing I ever stuck with, tried to do right, to the best of my many selves. And the people who came in, at first almost no one, later the crowds, were good people, people at their best, when they were in the Bookstore. I wish I'd still been living in it, instead of that broke-down cabin on the back side of the hill.

"I wish I'd died with the fucking books!" he yelled.

The man was in agony, bright black eyes desperate, a madman studying each of us for something no one had. Alas, the sad reality is, agony is the most common of emotions these days. The only thing to do is keep our silence, and give the man the floor.

"I heard it was a young guy, from one of those gangs ranging among the heaps on the other side of Eighteenth. So many rats over there. I grabbed Young Bob here—probably the best Bookstore clerk left until five days ago—and we went hunting. Took almost four days but we found him. He'd been bragging. Sooner or later they always brag. It's what they've got."

Booker went silent, stared out toward the broken empty street.

"What did you do with the punk, Booker?" asked Sky, ever one to cut to it.

"We killed him. Quick and painless."

"Then what?"

"Why, then we ate him. Of course."

"Eating the Bookstore arsonist is a reasonable form of justice," posited Bob. "A shame only in that we didn't have the proper background dining music. Perhaps a mix we used to play at Tsunami, back when there was electricity—the playlist called *Bob's Modern America* would have been appropriate. As usual, Shakespeare has been down this road before us. I am reminded of one of his early tragedies, *Titus Andronicus*, in which the main character addresses two evil young men whom, in an act of revenge for his daughter, he's about to cook up into pastry."

"How was he?" queried Old Rob, ever the curious connoisseur.

"Not good," said Booker. "Too much anger, spoils the meat. We probably should have cooked him. Likely rabid. And there was no marbling."

To that we all came alive.

"I need marbling," declared Shankar, speaking for the lot of us.

"And here it comes, boys, a steaming hot platter of meat, just the way you like it, well marbled and professionally singed," called Kate, bringing an official end to the last moment's holocaust of dismay.

"That's what I love about Turtles," said Booker, raising his head and coming around to the here and now. "Call it meat, call it whomever you want, may there always be marbling at Turtles. Amen!"

And with that we reached as one for the mounded platter of hot flesh, then fell back in our shaky seats and began to gnaw and gum with relish. Bob, still standing, grabbed a long greasy piece, added it to whatever was in the bloody hickory sack, then silently loped off, headed northeast, to the wreck of the former married student housing, to share with his partner Megan and their secret child, Molly, who loves her mother's watchful ways.

Whatever it was Kate served that night, at some point the whole gang began to bloat. The sludge at the bottom of the drink usually took care of it, and there was certainly no wise reason to complain about Kate's crew of scavengers. Still, something was amiss. And the worst thing was it still wasn't dark enough to be slinking off, each to our own little refuge, to shit or die alone.

Shankar, as usual the first to complain, let out a whiny groan. Unlike the rest of us, Old Shankar had always been stick-thin. For entertainment these days we sometimes watch his Adams apple when he swallows. Clearly, though, at the moment, to our alarm, we could see a lump writhing like a gigged rat in his taut bare belly, which he always kept naked, glowing in the gap between five unbuttoned suit coats.

"Meat and booze, meat and booze, every night it's meat and booze," he cried. "I take the leftovers home to my mom. It's killing her. We need vegetables, roots, rosemary, grape leaves, something!"

"I just don't shit anymore," said Sky. "And it's fine."

"If I still felt like doing some kitchen work," deadpanned Rob, "I'd be out digging camas root right this minute. Perfect time to do it, out in the cold wet dusk of a summer's eve. And the best place to dig them is just down the hill, at the end of the Twenty-Seventh Avenue slough, on the low flats of Amazon Creek, over to the drain side of what used to be the dog park. Fucking leash laws."

Old Rob, whose every story these days leads to the leash laws. A guaranteed laugh.

What else did we have?

"That's a lot of talk," snapped Old Dennis, a vegetarian back in the days of choice. "You go down there tonight. Go right ahead. But I'm telling you, you don't want to mess with those wild folk live in the jungle around Amazon Creek. They take full claim of that camas swale. Them and that tribe of old women who live on the other side, on the edge of the wetlands. You go down there, we'll be up here laughing, choking on the smoke of the fire your skinny ass is cooking in."

"I don't care about skinny, I'll bet there's still some marbling," drawled Booker, looking down towards Rob's withers, to a hoot and a holler from everyone present—who, if it came to a choice, would rather laugh than shit.

"I wouldn't have any problem scoring on camas root, if I wanted," bragged Rob. "I'm tight with those crazies. How it happened is I made friends with that dog of theirs, the only dog this side of the big river. And you know what they did to dogs on the other side. Ha!"

The clouds broke for a moment, Rob's face a bright pink in the gathering dusk.

"That's the meanest mongrel ever lived. Never barks, just bites. Never known a leash. And there I was, got it rolled over, lolling, me rubbing its belly, when they swarmed me. Fortunately, they saw my natural skill with the critter and brought me in. They had just come from a goose hunt down by the old sports field. We scrambled over to the old Sundance rubble, got a bonfire going out of some secret horde of actual firewood. And then the old women came out, and some young ones too, in their fifties and early sixties. They had every kind of vegetable. Some even looked garden grown. And that one old woman, with those beautiful white curls hanging almost to the ground . . ."

"There's a lot of old women fit that description," interrupted Booker, who as a bookseller had known many women well, which is reason enough to love the books.

"You know who I'm talking about," said Old Rob. "She's got the presence, like an old-fashioned Marian the Librarian. Someone we imagined loving when we were young. Strong and intelligent, calm and happy, upright and compassionate, hand in hand. You know the one, she's got a full smile, shows every tooth left, doesn't care about the gaps. Bright with an inner glow. Why, just seeing her smile will make your insignificant day in hell as good as it's ever going to be.

"She plays the fiddle, had it in the one hand, the other hand pulling a huge pot, more like a cauldron, on a two-wheel dolly, and it was full of camas root. Right away she took charge of cooking the stew, there in the rubble, pot after pot, the whole night long, camas root and vegetables and fresh-killed goose seasoned with everything that grows between the Amazon Creek and Pioneer Cemetery. Strange, they didn't have any liquor, but they had a lot of 'shrooms and an amazing variety of hot teas. Everyone played an instrument, be it a wooden spoon on a clay bowl, and I sang and danced with the dog. Although it wasn't the dog I woke up next to come late morning, warm and rested, needing to take a good country dump a long way from the nest."

Must have been the thought of the dump, because Old Rob suddenly broke out in a long hard laugh, displaying his full set of hand-carved mahogany teeth, reflecting the grey light of the ever-present rain.

Normally, we would have gladly shared in his merriment. But everyone knew, or at least knew the legend of the woman he was talking about. And the knowing quieted us, each for our own good reasons.

They call her Possum Killer, the name always spoken with deep reverence. None of us remember her other name from the way-back.

And that's as it should be. But every man and every woman has ever known her, somehow adores her, likely including her ex, whom I wouldn't be surprised to be the so-named Possum. Something about the mix of human in her, neither man nor woman would ever think a hurtful thought about her, even if her solitary, noble quest sometimes causes her to do things that might not meet general approval.

But fuck a bunch of approval! What she knows, and what she does, is everything for everyone at this end of what was once a town, then a city, now who knows what; everything, even if it's only the stories we hear through these long years of sorrow and separation, a most precious being, one of many who must still be out there somewhere, who give a moment's sweet meaning to the mostly dead thing called home.

And just as we love her, each in our own oddly perfect ways, there was also a quiet certainty among us that she wasn't the woman old Rob woke up next to, full of a healthy desire for a memorable shit. No way! More likely she simply knew some woman who wanted him way back when, and simply set them up. As is, Rob always speaks with a hint of riddle and half-truth, like the sound a violin tuned to fiddle makes when the goose is cooked with camas.

And then in the silence we heard it. Even Bill and Kate, in the dark hole of the bar, heard it. Even the crew by the fire in the alley heard it, came walking through the hole in the wall where the kitchen used to be, and joined us by the wide-open front of Turtles, overlooking what will never again be Willamette Street. From our perch we looked east, down what had once been the Twenty-Seventh Avenue throughway, now a roaring summer freshet. The sky stubbornly held a cold drizzling breath of dim grey, which proved just enough light to see an honest-to-goodness parade of scraggly shadows heading up the incline on our side of the blessed stream. At the front of the crowd, someone with white hair to the ground, a beacon in the last hint of light fading behind College Hill. For a moment there appeared the remnant glow of an old one's smile.

Then we heard it again. The single screech of a fiddle.

It harkened the time to break up for the night, to grovel back to our lonely burrows, which is the only way to truly be safe when the world is coming to an end. But there we all were, at the front porch of the shell of Turtles, facing east, watching, hoping, waiting. Ready.

CONTRIBUTORS

Ken Babbs is the author of Tsunami Press's inaugural title, *Cronies, a Burlesque: Adventures with Ken Kesey, Neal Cassady, the Merry Pranksters and the Grateful Dead.* Ohio-bred and Ohio-born, he is a graduate of Miami University in Oxford, Ohio, and a member of two NCAA tournament basketball teams. He attended graduate school at Stanford University, where he met Ken Kesey, Wendell Berry and other luminaries in Wallace Stegner's writing class. Five years in the Marine Corps followed, serving as a helicopter pilot, with his final tour of duty in Vietnam. He got off the chopper and onto the bus, *Further,* for the famous trip to Madhattan in 1964, chronicled in print by Tom Wolfe and filmed and taped by the Merry Pranksters. He shared forty-three years of collaboration and shenanigans with Kesey—doing shows, speaking engagements and musical cata-strophes—plus writing books, magazine articles, and co-editing six issues of *Spit in the Ocean.* Babbs co-wrote *Last Go Round* with Kesey, and went on to publish a novel based on his experiences in Vietnam, *Who Shot the Water Buffalo?* Married to a retired high school English teacher, he lives on a six-acre farm in the foothills of the Cascade Mountains in Oregon.

Elly Bookman grew up in downtown Atlanta, attended Colby College, and earned an MFA from the University of North Carolina at Greensboro, where she worked as a lecturer. Since 2013 she has worked as a full-time middle grade educator while consistently publishing her poetry in some of the most widely-read markets in the country, including *The New Yorker*, *Paris Review*, and *The American Poetry Review.* She was the recipient of the first annual Stanley Kunitz Memorial Prize from The American Poetry Review and the Lorraine Williams poetry prize from *The Georgia Review.* In 2016 she returned to her hometown where she currently teaches at the Paideia School.

Transplant to the Willamette Valley from the Great-Lakes state—back almost fifty years—**Deb Casey** has become a complete convert to the rivers, especially the McKenzie, where she and family often refresh. Visual/verbal marker, maker, mum, gram and big book-fan, she delights in painting with her youngest pals, plus mingling with other writers, readers, creative-sorts, traversing Pisgah trails at least once most weeks the past three decades: familiar turf!

Bob Craven is a poet, musician, and teacher born in Ellwood City, PA. Bob worked as a Tsunami Books clerk for several years, beginning in 2017. He studies working-class Appalachian culture from environmental and historical perspectives. He wrote the dissertation *Appalachian Moderns: Poetry and Music, 1936-1947* (2022) and the article "Documenting the Corporate Underworld in Mark Nowak's *Coal Mountain Elementary*" (2020). He teaches at Westminster College (New Wilmington, PA) as an Assistant Professor.

Brian Cutean, aka Brian QTN, Oregon songpoet and wordsmith musician, tours the country performing offbeat and touching observations on the socialography of the human condition and multilayered guitar melodies. His work is filled with conscious wordplay meta-fables that roll off the tongue, folky jazz melodies with an Alt-Roma blues beat and wordless guitar stylings. He has performed his songs of spirit and whimsy all over these United States for many years and has released 10 albums of original music. His first book, *Logodaidalia*, featuring "bedtime stories for when you get up," has just been released.

Bronwynn Dean is a writer and artist living on the Oregon Coast. Easily influenced by the moon and the tides, in her current incarnation, she is living her siren's dream of having a flower and art shop in a quaint coastal village and trying hard not to drown sailors.

Matthew Dickman is the award-winning author of *Husbandry, Wonderland, Mayakovsky's Revolver* and *All-American Poem*, winner of the May Sarton award from the American Academy of Arts and Sciences. He lives in Portland, Oregon.

In some circle of the COVID-19 pandemic, the day smoke from the Holiday Farm Fire cleared, **S.G. Ellerhoff** found himself, masked behind Tsunami's drink bar, cleaning used books. Three years a bookstore clerk and associate editor for Tsunami Press, he holds a

PhD from the School of English at Trinity College Dublin. He has authored and edited short stories, academic articles, and books of fiction, literary criticism, and natural history. His next book, a monograph, is *Jung and the Mythology of Star Wars*. More about his published work can be found at www.sgellerhoff.com.

Cecelia Hagen is a long-time Eugene resident and fan and patron of Tsunami Books. When she's not reading she's hiking Mt. Pisgah, or dancing tango, and doing things with her grandkids. Her book *Entering* (Airlie Press) and chapbook *Among Others* (Traprock Books) are often available at the bookstore.

Over the past four decades, Nebula- and Stoker Award-winning writer **Nina Kiriki Hoffman** has sold adult and young adult novels and more than 350 short stories. Her works have been finalists for the World Fantasy, Mythopoeic, Sturgeon, Philip K. Dick, and Endeavour awards. Nina does production for *The Magazine of Fantasy & Science Fiction*. She teaches writing through Fairfield County Writers' Studio and Wordcrafters in Eugene. She lives in Oregon. For Nina's publications, visit her website here: ofearna.us/books/hoffman.html.

Meli Hull writes about interpersonal relationships and ADHD. She lives in Eugene, Oregon, with her husband, small daughter, and two cats. She used to work at Tsunami Books; now she works as a library clerk. Because of this, her special pub trivia niche is knowing the titles and authors of many books she's never read in addition to the titles and authors of all the ones she has read.

Valerie Ihsan, Story Analyst and Coach, is the author of *You Can't Dance a Lie: A Memoir of Stepping Into My Truth*, *The Scent of Apple Tea*, and *Smell the Blue Sky: Young, Pregnant, and Widowed*, winner of a B.R.A.G. Medallion for Top Indie-Published Books. She co-chaired the Eugene Chapter of Willamette Writers for over eight years, diagnoses manuscripts as a Certified Three Story Method Editor, and helps authors write memoirs. She podcasts at the Writer Craft Podcast, loves dogs and aims to live in Costa Rica and run writing retreats. She lives in Oregon with her husband and three dogs.

Scott Landfield has been a worker and owner of Tsunami Books for twenty-seven years. His parents each owned bookstores in the Midwest at times in their lives between newspaper work. Scott came to Oregon in 1978 to plant trees. Over a twenty-year career he planted over 2 million trees, while taking the summers off to be with his daughter. At present he works too many hours at the bookstore to finish any of the books he has spent his adult life writing.

Jorah LaFleur is a writer/performer who enjoys wearing many different hats. She finds herself on stage as a spoken word poet, event emcee, and actor. Offstage, she works with youth as a teaching artist. Jorah is currently serving as the lead Writer in Residence at the 501(c)(3) nonprofit Wordcrafters in Eugene. She is committed to helping others experience the power of being seen/heard, and to promoting the arts as tools of social change, and community building. Connect with her at jorahlafleur.com.

Dorianne Laux's sixth collection, *Only As the Day is Long: New and Selected Poems*, was named a finalist for the 2020 Pulitzer Prize for Poetry. Her fifth collection, *The Book of Men*, was awarded the Paterson Prize. Her fourth book of poems, *Facts About the Moon* won the Oregon Book Award and was short-listed for the Lenore Marshall Poetry Prize. Laux is also the author of *Awake*; *What We Carry*, a finalist for the National Book Critic's Circle Award; *Smoke*; as well as a fine small press edition, *The Book of Women*. She is the co-author of the celebrated text *The Poet's Com-panion: A Guide to the Pleasures of Writing Poetry*.

Michael McGriff is a former Tsunami Books clerk, book buyer, jingling scrapper, and proud toilet scrubber (not necessarily in that order). He's also a native of Coos Bay, Oregon, where much of his writing is centered. His books include the poetry collections *Eternal Sentences, Black Postcards, Early Hour, Home Burial,* and *Dismantling the Hills;* the short story collection *Our Secret Life in the Movies;* a translation of Tomas Tranströmer's *The Sorrow Gondola;* and an edition of David Wevill's essential writing, *To Build My Shadow a Fire.* He directs the Creative Writing Program at the University of Idaho.

Carter McKenzie is the author of the chapbook of poetry *Naming Departure* (Traprock Books, 2004), and two full-length collections of poetry: *Out of Refusal* (Airlie Press, 2010) and *Stem of Us* (Flowstone Press, 2018). She is an active member of the Springfield-Eugene chapter of SURJ (Showing Up for Racial Justice).

Joseph Millar's newest, *Dark Harvest: Selected Poems*, came out from Carnegie Mellon University Press in 2021. His work has won fellowships from the NEA and the Guggenheim Foundation.

Mose Tuzik Mosley is a writer, carpenter and pretty good guy. Currently concentrating on travel writing, he will have an anthology of his latest work, *A Journey With Orvis*, published spring 2024 by Island Earth Press. He lives in Eugene, Oregon, and Los Cabos, BCS, Mexico.

Erik Muller (1941-2021) was a life-long poet and poetry advocate. He thought of W. C. Williams and Wallace Stevens as his 'grandfathers.' Born in New York City, he settled in Oregon with his family in 1969. In addition to publishing many of his own books of poetry and poetry criticism, such as *And Yet: Selected Poems*, *A New Text of the World: A Reader's Guide to Wallace Stevens*, and *Durable Goods*, he was an ardent supporter of other local poets. One of the founders and editors of the journal *Fireweed: Poetry of Western Oregon*, he also published two chapbook series: Coos Writers Series and Traprock Books.

Eve Müller recently moved from College Park, Maryland, to Eugene, Oregon, with her cat and sweetheart. She has published in *Sequestrum*, *The Writing Disorder*, *Thieving Magpie*, and *Empty House*. When she is not writing lyrical memoir and autobiographical fiction, she bakes cakes, spends time with her two wildling daughters, conducts research on autism and language, and skinny-dips whenever/wherever she can.

Emily Poole is a natural history illustrator based in Eugene, Oregon. She received her BFA in Illustration from the Rhode Island School of Design and has created work for numerous organizations, including the National Museum of Wildlife Art, Sasquatch Books,

Oregon Country Fair, and *High Country News*. Emily began working at Tsunami Books in 2016 and has thus far painted two murals for the bookstore building. Her art can be found at www.epooleart.com.

D.S. Rhodes was born in Chicago in the mid-Sixties and grew up playing saxophone and baseball. He studied English Lit. at UC Berkeley and Northwestern University, facing "*What are you going to do with that?!*" from family and friends. He moved to Eugene in 1993 and, after academia didn't pan out, did what all English majors secretly dream of doing: he opened a bookstore—Tsunami Books. In 2008, he moved to Hawaii to decompress, work on an organic farm, and explore musical and literary creativity. He currently resides in New Mexico—the Land of Enchantment—where stories suddenly started flowing out as fast as they could be written down, mostly speculative future fiction and YA fantasy, as yet unpublished.

Jenny Root is a poet, editor and event planner in Eugene, Oregon. Her poems have appeared in *About Place Journal, basalt, CIRQUE, Cloudbank, Crab Creek Review, Fireweed, Windfall*, and in the anthology, *New Poets of the American West*. Her full-length collection, *The Company of Sharks*, was published in 2013. Jenny was an employee at Tsunami Books from 1996 to 2000. In that time, she organized and hosted many readings, including the all-night Poetry Filibuster and tours of Oregon Book Awards finalists. A fellow of PLAYA, a past co-host of the Springfield Poetry Reading Series, and past director of the Lane Literary Guild, she now enjoys coordinating an annual writers retreat at Tipi Village Retreat in Marcola, Oregon.

Maxine Scates is the author of three previous collections of poetry, *Undone, Black Loam*, and *Toluca Street*. She is coeditor, with David Trinidad, of *Holding Our Own: The Selected Poems of Ann Stanford*. Her poems have appeared widely in such journals as the *American Poetry Review, Agni*, the *New Yorker, Ploughshares*, and *Poetry*. Her poetry is the recipient of two Pushcart Prizes, the Agnes Lynch Starrett Poetry Prize, and the Oregon Book Award for Poetry.

Tom A. Titus is a runner, forager, father, grandfather, amphibian biologist, and free-range philosopher who writes at the messy interface of human experience and the natural world. Miraculously, he managed to corral divergent paths in music, education, and biology into a career in evolutionary genetics. He finally graduated by retiring as a research biologist at the University of Oregon. Tom has authored three books of essays. His most recent work, *Dancing with an Apocalypse*, is an attentive response to the pandemic years of 2020 and 2021, inspired by neighborhood newts, a hovering raven, wind in old trees, and a decaying house in the Coast Range. His writing has also appeared in the collections *Forest Under Story* and *Medicine for a Nightmare*, and periodicals such as *Oregon Quarterly Magazine* and *Turtle Island Quarterly*. Tom is a co-creator of The Nature of Gratitude, a program of poetry, prose, music, and spoken word celebrating our grateful presence in the world. He loves bourbon straight, coffee he can spread on toast, and writing that makes him laugh and cry, preferably at the same time. When he's feeling spunky, Tom blogs at Words on the Nature of Life, which can be found at tomtitus.substack.com.

John Witte grew up in New England, the son of Polish immigrants. His poems have appeared widely, in publications such as *The New Yorker*, *Paris Review*, *Kenyon Review*, and *American Poetry Review*, and been included in *The Norton Introduction to Literature*. He is the author of *Loving the Days* (Wesleyan University Press, 1978), *The Hurtling* (Orchises Press, 2005), *Second Nature* (University of Washington Press, 2008), *Disquiet* (University of Washington Press, 2015), and *All That Matters Now* (Lynx House Press, 2022). For thirty years he was the editor of *Northwest Review*. The recipient of two fellowships from the National Endowment for the Arts, he taught Ecopoetry and other subjects at the University of Oregon in Eugene, where he lives on the outskirts of town with his family.

Kelsey Yoder is a writer and educator living in Colorado Springs, Colorado. Her fiction has appeared in *Five Points: A Journal of Literature and Art* and other literary magazines. She worked at Tsunami Books from 2015 to 2016.